CHARLOTTE
Haulin' Around Town
Streetside 1950 – 1963

Illuminating places of long ago, vignettes, never published photos — All in a journey into a special time in Charlotte.

CHARLOTTE
Haulin' Around Town
Streetside 1950 – 1963

Illuminating places of long ago, vignettes, never published photos — All in a journey into a special time in Charlotte.

by
Earl G. Gulledge

This document is copyrighted by Earl G. Gulledge ©2025

All rights reserved. No part of this publication may be reproduced, distributed, or transmitted in any form or by any means, including photocopying, recording, or other electronic or mechanical methods, without the prior written permission of the publisher, except in the case of brief quotations embodied in critical reviews and certain other noncommercial uses permitted by copyright law. For permission requests, write to the publisher, addressed "Attention: Permissions Coordinator," at the address below.

ISBN: 979-8-89933-004-9 (Paperback)
Library of Congress Control Number: 2025945694
Printed in the United States of America.
First printing 2025.

Redhawk Publications
The Catawba Valley Community College Press
2550 Hwy 70 SE
Hickory, NC 28602
https://redhawkpublications.com

Layout and Design by Melanie Johnson Zimmermann

Special Thanks for Their Contributions

Melvin D. Carson

Patsy Barnett McKinsey

Russ Rodgers, Jr.

Richard Sharpe

Sam Smith

Table of Contents

Preface 9
Introduction   1950 - 1963 11
Lay of The Land 15
- About the City
- About Me
- Sum of the Parts

2. A Kid of Six, Eight, Ten 23
- Adventures With My Father
- Park Avenue/Wilmore
- Graham Street/Statesville Avenue
- The Missile Plant
- US 74 East Independence Boulevard/ Monroe Road
- North Tryon
- Wilkinson Boulevard
- Central Avenue

3. Adventures Streetside: Downtown and Elsewhere 57
- The Square – Downtown
- By Myself In The Big City
- Streetside – Tryon and Trade Streets

4. Charlotte's Premiere Street 91
- Independence Boulevard

5. Airport and Environs 113
- Douglas Municipal Airport
- Terminals
- Airline Operations

6. Trains, Buses, and Cabs – But No Boats 131
- Railroads
- Duke Power/City Coach Lines
- Intercity Buses
- Taxis

7. Schools, Churches, and Other Places 163
   + Memorial Stadium
   + Ovens Auditorium/Coliseum
   + Lots of Other Places

8. Movies and Other Things 185
   + My Favorite Places - Theaters
   + Lifestyles, Radio, and Becoming a "Ham"

9. Streetwise 203
   + Life Skills and Learning

10. Retrospective 207

Bibliography 212

About the Author 213

Preface

I was in a new tower uptown attending a continuing education luncheon for credits needed for maintenance of my NC architectural license. Standing on a veranda with my host I pointed out an old but still identifiable former railroad right-of-way in the center of the city. Just another conversation about Charlotte covering things few seem to know or remember. I spent a great amount of time "on the streets" in my childhood. My memory is long and deep. This is my contribution documenting places and lifestyles during my youth in Charlotte in the 1950s and early 1960s.

So many conversations seem eventually to reach a point about Charlotte's immediate past and "what was somewhere before what is there now". With so many new residents, there is an understandable and unending curiosity about Charlotte's history. There are many books that depict Charlotte and its past vis a vis the present. I have a unique perspective of growing up in Charlotte. I want to share it with others and document it for the future. My commentary is derived from streetside experience of the places and events of the years that defined my childhood. I have included a unique granularity of detail.

The period 1950 until 1963 was an extraordinary time to grow up in our city. Charlotte kept its pre-WWII identity, life, and urban appearance until just after the Korean War, 1950-1953. Visible change began with the post Korean War economic expansion.

New residential growth and declining public transit ridership produced more vehicles on our streets; the beginning of suburban shopping centers changed how we lived, and rapid growth altered visual landscapes as I moved from childhood into and through teenage years. I had so many adventures, and they were framed directly by the indelible memory of people/buildings/places in Charlotte.

This narrative journey will visit important aspects of Charlotte's lifestyle, its people, and notable/important places. From time to time my adventures and experiences may wander through time and location. Where needed, I will explain the social context of topics. Virtual journeys will follow North Graham Street/Statesville Avenue, US 74 /Independence Boulevard/Monroe Road, North Tryon Street, Wilkinson Boulevard, and Central

Avenue. We will explore downtown in detail. We will delve deeply into transportation – planes, buses, cabs, and trains. A complete chapter will chronicle Independence Boulevard. Theaters were a big part of my lifestyle and will also be covered in detail.

Looking backwards in time modulates the difficulties one may have encountered and puts a mellow overlay on things that at one time were perhaps considered with less fondness. Life during my childhood was not nearly as sanguine as many of my generation wistfully remember decades afterwards. The "good old days" in part may have been functions of our unencumbered youthful minds and our often-simplistic lifestyles of the 1950s. One cannot reasonably explore 1950 to 1963 without deference to the social/economic dynamics that were operative then. We were a society with specific demarcations reflecting economics, education, race, housing, and amenities. Honest commentary on society and culture demands recognition of those realities, that even in my youth, were easily discernable. There were many questions for which I had no answers, and often in conflict with the virtues I learned at home, in school, and in church. Context is everything, and I will attempt to keep things in context as I saw it.

Allow me to note that maps may be inaccurate for the time they are dated. Cartographers often include rights-of-way of known future construction. Therefore, documentation on some maps may be inaccurate based on their publication dates

Importantly, sometimes public narratives may also be less than accurate, and that information may enter our conversations as truth. And much like misinformation on the internet, it soon passes as fact. A few years ago, local news covered a dispute between a lessor and lessee on the city's west side. The offended party complained about gentrification of the former Black neighborhood of Enderly Park. Enderly Park was a white residential area from its beginning to decades later. Many friends lived there. This happens when assumptions are made without facts. I have written what I saw and heard. I have tried to validate locations, and corroborated details and other information with available resources.

Introduction 1950 - 1963

The young people of my generation indeed hauled around town, usually in their family's single automobile, quite often walking as it was for me, riding bikes, and of course riding city buses. I was fortunate to see Charlotte from street level. This is my contribution to preserving what I lived during a definable, transitory time.

My objective is to present a definitive narrative of Charlotte from 1950 until 1963 by focusing on and identifying the places and society in Charlotte that framed my life. My intent is neither to offer a definitive history of Charlotte nor to track the chronology of every street, neighborhood, business, venue, and notable person. This commentary is not predicated on geographic or any other considerations but rather based on where I went, what I did, and what I saw, heard, and learned. Those adventures fold into places, many gone but some remaining, that are important, and I think worth remembering.

In 1963 I was, except for voting, afforded the privileges of adulthood at age eighteen. My interests, experiences and pursuits were changing. And so was our nation.

I was five years old when 1950 presented a new decade. The post WWII world was being changed forever by a decade's long standoff with the Soviet Union, coined "The Cold War" by Barnard Baruch. The Korean War would only briefly delay the explosive growth for Americans – my parents' generation - who had weathered both the Great Depression and WWII.

After the surprise launch of Sputnik 1 by the Soviet Union in 1957, the nation was in shock. Like many of my friends, I wanted to become an engineer and be part of the race to beat the Russians into space, the moon and beyond. It was part of a national obsession. Dedicated teachers motivated us to make the most of our education in preparation to take the nation further to greatness. Heady stuff indeed.

I graduated from high school in 1963 and was ready to begin at Charlotte College (now UNC-C), to study engineering. According to musical purists it was the final year for rock 'n' roll music before the so-called "British Invasion". Shortly after high school graduation my father traded our 1954 Ford two door Custom Line for a black 1961 Ford Galaxie Victoria.

The summer of '63 was sweet. All was well until that sunny November Friday in Dallas when President John Kennedy's energetic voice was suddenly silenced by an assassin's bullet. The event slammed into the euphoric optimism that many of us felt toward our futures.

For the sixties the election of youthful John F. Kennedy was indeed a benchmark that reflected the optimism and upward outlook of the nation. Kennedy died on November 22, 1963. The next day the depressing long, slow drawl of President Lyndon Johnson told me it was over, the nation was going to another place. Oswald's bullets started a decades-long chain of interrelated events. We each had our pursuits and careers; the halcyon days of the fifties rapidly faded from collective consciousness. I trust our journey will offer readers a definitive look at mid-twentieth century places and life as experienced by a young boy at street level — *Charlotte - Haulin' Around Town.*

Chapter Notes

President Lyndon Johnson: Johnson was a Texas Senator and master political operative in a time when political compromise was the norm and produced beneficial legislation. He was by some accounts marginalized by the Kennedys.

Johnson, a deal maker who knew how to accomplish goals, did not possess the public comportment and stage presence of John F. Kennedy. Kennedy was youthful compared to Dwight Eisenhower whom he succeeded, and Johnson was hardly a motivator like JFK. Presidents, then, addressed the nation on important matters and Johnson's style was hardly uplifting.

Johnson is most remembered for the Vietnam War, a foreign policy war of choice born in the "containment" era of the Cold War. His extraordinary domestic accomplishments included Medicare, Civil Rights Act of 1964, and Voting Rights Act of 1965. He announced in March of 1968 he would not seek re-election thereby creating a path for former Vice-President Richard Nixon, who lost to JFK in 1960, to finally reach the Oval Office in 1969 by defeating Hubert H. Humphrey, VP to LBJ.

The Vietnam War continued until January 15, 1973, when offensive operations ended in Vietnam and US forces were withdrawn. South Vietnam was finally overwhelmed by North Vietnamese forces on April 30, 1975, and Vietnam was one nation again and our national nightmare was over at a huge cost in lives and national treasure.

The Contradiction. This advertisement from 1948 is remarkable. In its fine print it proudly announced its wait staff. Assuming the words were intended to be complimentary of a group whose performances were the epitome of their calling, they would have to ride in the rear of a city bus if that were their means of transportation to their jobs. Interestingly, in reflection of reality, the movies of the forties and fifties (and railroad ad photos) always had Black men in the roles of Pullman porters and dining car waiters.

Chapter 1
The Lay of The Land

The Basics

1950 was more than a mid-century point. Charlotte was poised to assume a bigger presence in the South. The 1950 census counted a few more than 134,000 residents. Business, professional, and retail services were, with only a few exceptions, concentrated downtown (yes, it was called downtown in 1950) and near the hospitals along the eastern outer ring of the urban center. The terminal buildings for Douglas Municipal Airport were former military operations buildings at what was still often called Morris Field – a large Army Air Forces training base during WWII. The Armory Auditorium was the town's largest venue. Intercity buses like Trailways and Greyhound Lines were an accepted and popular means of intercity travel. City buses were operated by Duke Power Company and were everywhere. As Bill Finger, former Assistant Director of Charlotte Department of Transportation, once related at a brown bag luncheon, being located on a bus route was considered an asset in the purchase or sale of a home. P&N Railway still ran interurban cars between Gastonia and Charlotte.

Entertainment choices were somewhat limited, as one might expect for the time. Movies, bowling, and skating were popular. There were, of course, golf courses and driving ranges. I was a teenager before I can recall knowing anyone who played golf. Movie theaters were popular as they were air-conditioned at a time when some of the taller buildings uptown were not. Other than replicating cowboy "B" movies in my grandmother's backyard, options to movies were visits with my father to either the airport or the Southern Railway Depot on West Trade Street. Both locations inculcated a love of airplanes and trains that solidified in my being. A real treat was the Wilkinson Boulevard Dairy Queen. Revolution Park pool was an on/off option depending on the status of polio cases. In 1952, the worst of the national polio epidemics took 3,145 lives out of 57,675 cases. When the Salk polio vaccine became available in 1955, there was no anti-vax movement, and we all hastened to get our vaccinations. Conspiracy theorists of that time had not discovered vaccines and were trying to convince the populace that our government was filled with communists. The fear of polio was real, and all of us received our vaccinations as quickly as we could get them.

1950 was pivotal for other important reasons. On June 25, North Korean forces of KIM Il Sung, grandfather of Kim Jung Un, crossed the 38th Parallel, starting the Korean War. I thought that any day an army truck would appear in front of my grandmother's house and my father (inactive reservist) would go out and get in with a squad of other men and be gone. The Soviet Union had exploded its first nuclear weapon in 1949. And a new technology that would replace radio as the primary communication/entertainment medium was on the scene – television. Soon, a post-Korean War proliferation of new automobiles would feed rapid suburbanization, which included housing developments, streets, new schools, and shopping centers.

On this rapidly changing landscape, my peers and I played, learned, and grew up. For the longest time, Charlotte had been a booster city, tearing down older things and replacing them with newer ones. A prominent local historian later commented that "Charlotte's commitment to preservation is a mile wide and an inch deep." Fortunately, we have more respect and creativity in 2025 for our built heritage and work to preserve or rehabilitate older structures.

Often, I have been asked: "What was Charlotte like?" The answer: fun for me as the city seemed boundless. Charlotte, like all cities, was defined by buildings, places, and people and their activities. Charlotte was a city punctuated by quiet, distinct neighborhoods. To appreciate our narrative, it is essential to define how all these elements were distributed throughout Charlotte. I will present Charlotte as I saw it as a young boy.

About Me

My home life was a little different from that of most of my peers and imbued with some different experiences. My father and mother were married in March of 1942. In May, he was in the first group of the Eighth Air Force to deploy to England (go overseas as it was called). I was born in June 1945, after VE Day but while the Pacific War was still raging. After the war, he and my mother lived in her parents' home on State Street, a not-uncommon occurrence for young couples of that time. My mother met my father when

Chapter 1 - The Lay of The Land

she rode the No. 10 State Street bus route on which he was a driver. They were about to move into a new home on Woodruff Place, in Wesley Heights, when she passed away on Christmas Day 1948. She was organist for Wesley Heights Methodist Church and worked in the comptroller's office at the A&P offices (its top floor is now an event location) on West Bland Street (now Westmere Avenue). We lived with my grandparents for about three years.

Subsequently, in 1951, my father purchased a new house on Kimberly Road, which connected from Remount Road to West Boulevard - on the heights west of Irwin Creek. After the war, with his siblings married, his widowed mother, "Big Mama," moved to Florida for a full-time job as a practical nurse-caregiver in today's terminology. His mother later returned from Florida in August 1951 to live with us – something like Aunt Bea moving to Mayberry for Opie. As it turned out, we vacated our house in June of 1954. We occupied a rental house on Greene Street in what had become known as Ashley Park. "Big Mama," as my cousins called her, needed a couple of additional years to qualify for Social Security benefits, and she relocated back to Florida in the summer of 1955.

We moved into 2100 of the Weyland Avenue Apartments (it is still there and nicely maintained) for six months until we relocated to our final residence, a duplex on Marlowe Avenue near Berryhill Road. My grandmother then returned to Charlotte in January 1958 and remained with us until my father passed away in the summer of 1964. During the years she was away, I was in fact a "latch key child", a term I did not learn of until years later. Of course, I still had my mother's parents to support me.

Kimberly Road was populated mostly by WWII veterans. Our house was new; it cost just under $9,000 and was financed with a VA loan. Often called "GI loans" because they were structured for WWII veterans. Our home was not in a subdivision but on a new street adjacent to an existing residential area, where there had previously been woods. I believe all the houses had five rooms and a bath. The Krimmingers had two children, the Hinsons had four – I am not certain how they managed it in a small house. A classmate of my mother's, Coit Troutman – Harry P. Harding Class of 1938 - lived across the street from us. He was the pastor of Westover Baptist Church.

He drove an Oldsmobile 88 with V-8, and a Hydramatic transmission – I remember it well as I was easily impressed by the pricier trappings of capitalism.

Virtually all husbands worked. Contrary to their portrayal on television, many wives worked, often using skills learned during wartime employment. Duke Power Company owned the city bus system (until City Coach purchased it in 1955), which employed my father. He drove a bus almost from the time he moved to Charlotte from Morven, NC, in Anson County in 1939. He lived at the downtown YMCA and, for a while, worked for Charlotte Drug Co. (a pharmacy) at East Trade and South College Streets. A stroke of luck enabled him to connect with Mr. J.B. Ashe of Duke Power. Soon afterwards, he was a city bus driver, which was his only job there afterwards, except for time in the US Army Air Forces.

Sum of its Parts

Following WWII, Charlotte was a mix of single-family homes, duplexes, and a considerable number of quadraplexes. Housing demand after WWII outpaced housing growth, and aggregations of quadraplexes became a cost-effective way to create housing quickly and optimize land use. Charlotte was a segregated city – not only by race but also socio/economics and therefore education.

Some easily identifiable Black neighborhoods (but not all) were Southside Homes near South Tryon and Remount Road, Fairview Homes, Oaklawn/Double Oaks neighborhoods between Beattie's Ford Road and Statesville Avenue, Biddleville, Washington Heights near Johnson C. Smith University, Grier Heights, Cherry, and Brooklyn or Second Ward as it was often called from its clockwise geographic location as one of the City's four wards. It was not until the 1960s that I heard the term Black replace "colored," which was universal in the 1950s. There was a city pool for "colored" people, there were "colored" movie theaters, and there was a "colored" hospital.

White areas were (but not limited to) Elizabeth, Midwood, The Plaza, Wilmore, Dilworth, Park-Hutchinson, Hoskins, Glenwood, Eastover, Selwyn Avenue, Ashley Park, Avondale, Wesley Heights, Queens Road, and Belmont. Ashley Park was new on the west side, and the South Boulevard corridor was quickly developing with residential neighborhoods on its east side.

Chapter 1 - The Lay of The Land

My perception of racial separation at the time was simple: things are as they are, and I understood they were going to stay that way. It all seemed too complex to untangle. There was little political movement or activism in the fifties, which later happened in the sixties. The fact was, we were busy with schoolwork and thinking about our next semester. We had a strictly segregated education system. However, I never heard a remark or insinuation by a teacher that reflected poorly on any race.

By the time I was eleven or twelve, I had processed the cultural landscape and understood the attitudes and animosity toward Black people by many White people. It was deeply embedded in our culture. I could not reconcile how Black people could serve us food at school, take care of the elderly, serve in the military, and be treated as they were. It was illogical. When I was 13 or 14, I recall discussing segregation with a few friends. Like me, they were having difficulty understanding some societal norms. It was not until after high school that I began to engage with adults on the topic, and I was always a contrarian. The older generation seemed to always express their opinions with terminal finality and often under a religious mantra. Things were just too neat, too well packaged.

It did not take me long to learn that wealth – meaning money and education, expensive automobiles, and large homes – was concentrated elsewhere from where I lived. During the fifties, after Christmas Eve dinner, I would ride with my Aunt Margaret, Uncle Bob, and my grandparents (mother's parents) through Myers Park to view Christmas decorations. From East Boulevard to Queens Road, we would go to where the residents had the financial means for exterior decorations. Wealth was positioned geographically in Midwood, Eastover, Myers Park, Queens Road, and Selwyn Avenue. Neither I nor my family nor my friends considered ourselves "poor". We were just regular folks, and I was to somehow use education to go somewhere higher in my life than had others in my family. I did not comprehend what would be necessary to reach that distant point in my future, but I did know my father and thousands of others had fought a nasty war to preserve the country, and I was proud to be a beneficiary of it all.

Center City.

This photo was found in former American Credit Company files. A parade is in progress on Trade Street. Probably taken during either Veterans Day Parade or Shrine Bowl Parade in 1962, 63, 64. (The Christmas parade took place in late afternoons and followed Tryon Streets). The Selwyn Hotel building is still in place. NCNB and Cutter Building (201 S. Tryon) were completed in 1962. According to legend, each general contractor tried to wait out the other to see who pumped ground water first to lower the water table.

George King Cutter was a developer who was tried but not convicted of murdering his girlfriend. He passed away a couple of years afterwards. The building became the American Credit Building (owned by Wachovia). ACC was spun off in 1979 and sold to Barclays Bank. The company became known as BarclaysAmericanCorporation. The building was stripped down to its concrete structure (cantilevered waffle slab without exterior columns) about 2000 and rebuilt.

The former NCNB structure was also heavily renovated. Independence Building was imploded in October 1981. It was NC's first skyscraper in 1909 with two additional floors added in 1912. Wachovia Building at 129 West Trade was the first post-depression center city high rise structure in December 1957. Hotel Charlotte (top left beyond Wachovia and later named White House Inn) was imploded in TV special in 1987. Richard Nixon stayed there during his fall 1960 Presidential campaign. Photo: Author's collection.

Chapter Notes

"B" Westerns: Western movies were a Hollywood staple for decades. Films such as *Stagecoach, Red River, Shane,* and *The Searchers* are classic first-run film productions. The so-called "B" movies were less expensive productions and often were run a part of a double feature. They were usually shorter than the first-run films and had fewer top stars. They were in fact full movies and not serial westerns which were continuing stories that were shown weekly in many theaters at the same weekly time.

38th Parallel: Latitude 38 Degrees or the demarcation line between North and South Korea, is a resultant of WWII. The North, led by KIM Il Sung (grandfather of Kim Jong-Un) was aligned with the Soviet Union and China and at 4:00 a.m. on June 25, 1950, invaded South Korea. The United Nations engaged to defend the South, and the Korean War continued until July 27, 1953, when an armistice was executed with forces back in place along the 38th parallel as existed prior to the start of the war. South Korea was preserved and became a successful industrial democracy. There was a lot of anger within the US as it was thought by many that we did not win the war as we did in WWII. The world had changed and there was fear that a nuclear exchange with the Soviet Union might be a possibility. The war set the US on a policy of deterrence that fundamentally held the world order without another world war for the next 70 years – Pax Americana. A significant result of the conflict was the firing of Gen Douglas MacArthur by President Harry Truman. The war was one predicate for the "Red Scare" years fostered by Senator Joe McCarthy.

Polio statistics: US Public Health Service, CDC, as presented by website Our World in Data. The first polio vaccine was the Salk vaccine was developed by Jonas Salk and made available to the public in 1955. The Sabine vaccine was available about five years later.

Tryon Street

South Tryon looking north from between 3rd and 4th Streets. Auto at lower left is a 1946, '47, or '48 Mercury, so this photo portrays Charlotte's financial district as it would have looked in the late forties or early fifties. The structure in the center is the Liberty Life Building, built in 1927, and, at twenty stories, was the tallest in North and South Carolina. Underneath the Bank of Charlotte sign and at ground level is the marquee for the Imperial Theater. The Broadway Theater marquee is visible below the Thacker's Cafeteria vertical sign, and its then-current feature was a rerun of the 1939 Tyrone Power film Jesse James. Charles Spencer Photo.

Chapter 2
A Kid of Six, Eight, Ten……

Afternoons with My Father

In retrospect, it is more than remarkable how large virtually everything appeared when I was six or eight. The city seemed huge and almost any travel within it was an adventure. I was about to learn the city well.

Nothing was accomplished, transacted, or purchased online. Transactions for commerce, excepting teletypes and Western Union telegrams, were in person, by delivery service, or by US Mail. Credit cards were written up at gas stations on receipt pads. In the 1930s through the 1960s, department stores used metal Charga-Plates, which looked somewhat like military dog tags, to imprint purchases on triplicate receipt pads. It would be 1968 before I had my first "plastic" money – a BankAmerica card. My father never had a bank card, but I remember he did have gas company cards.

When I was six, my father would arrive home about 3:30 p.m., having gone to work for the Duke Power bus system about 5:30 a.m. He would have errands that were engaged in commerce of some kind, and I almost always went with him. We stayed in the geographic bounds of an area from South Boulevard to West Morehead Street.

In my youth, it was seemingly an unending universe of places, people, and captivating things.

Park Avenue/Wilmore and Surroundings

Our destination would be somewhere in the South Boulevard corridor, often along East Park Avenue between South Boulevard and Camden Road. Park Avenue was unique, something of a predecessor for the types of retail services we see embedded in contemporary mixed-use developments. A & P at 100 East Park was a major national grocery chain and occupied the still extant territorial style building on the south side of Park Avenue adjacent to the Southern Railway tracks. Elsewhere on the street was about everything one might need. Adjacent to the tracks on the north side of Park was the Doggett Lumber Company at 111. Between there and South Boulevard were the following: a Radio-TV shop, a Furniture/Jewelry store, Park Avenue

Barber Shop, a Beauty Shop, a Billiards parlor, Southern 5 & 10, and Niven Drugs. On the opposite side: A&P, Coney Island Grill, Tadlock's Shoe Repair, Park Avenue Hardware and Seed, and Kin Harry Laundry. Some of the storefronts were later preserved and integrated into new development.

There was a sliver of property between the Southern Railway tracks and Camden Road on the north side of Park Avenue, enough land to accommodate a small grill – Little Rock Lunch. Often, after I had made a purchase at the dime store, my father would park in the postage-stamp-sized parking lot and have a beer before we headed home. The Columbia Division Southern Railway tracks were only a few feet away. Before the cutoff near Steel Creek Road was constructed around Charlotte in 1954, there was a chance I might have seen diesel freight coming in from Columbia! Today, the little parking area is the dining patio for the Flower Child eatery. Across Camden Road was Watson's laundry at 100 West Park. Many folks did not have washing machines, so Watson's and many other laundries around town were a necessity. Park Avenue heading west was filled with homes. Transitional zoning was unknown then.

Just to the south on Camden Road was Dilworth Poultry (later Price's Chicken Coop). It became a Charlotte icon and closed in 2021. At one time, Dilworth Poultry sold dressed chickens. I recall that my father would occasionally pay them a visit to pick up a freshly dressed hen – my grandmother called them pullets - for his mother to prepare. In later years, it was famous for its fried chicken. Like the Coffee Cup on South Clarkson Street, Price's was an iconic establishment with a long history that is no longer part of our streetscape.

On the northeast corner of South Boulevard. (1533) and Park Avenue was Harris Hart, a clothing store that featured quality furnishings for men, women, and children comparable to Belk. Hart, in fact, survived until the seventies. A CVS resides there today. Next to Dilworth Sundries, located at 1601, was the Dilworth Theater at 1609. The Dilworth scored a major coup when it played Cleopatra, which showed for months. Sometime around 1953, a new dime store named Crest opened at 1620 South Boulevard A new source for toys and models was a welcome addition to my father's errand route. Hankins and Whittington Funeral Directors were located at 1714 South Boulevard, before later moving to their present East Boulevard

Chapter 2 - A Kid of Six, Eight, Ten......

location. Nearby at 1719 South Boulevard was Weathers Furniture Company. Interestingly, it was still an active business in the 1970s, and its building still survives. In 1976, my wife and I purchased a Thomasville dining room ensemble from Bob Weathers, and he was indeed still very much a super salesman. The Park Avenue area businesses were representative of similar perimeter groupings on Central Avenue, in North Charlotte, and on Providence Road.

As it turned out Hankins and Whittington became indelible in my memory. Just a few houses away from us on Kimberly Road lived the Burns family. The father, an electrician, had died by accidental electrocution in 1950. Mrs. Burns had three children: Jerry, 14, Carl, 12, and Joyce, 10. Their mother was a day shift supervisor with Southern Bell on Caldwell Street downtown. During the Christmas vacation, the children had lots of free time and apparently were unsupervised on December 30, 1953. George and Grace met two friends, both boys, at a pond on the north side of West Boulevard just off Watson Drive. It was a short distance west of the Remount Road and West Boulevard intersection, and had posted "No Trespassing" signs. Carl and one friend got into a small boat that had been left unattended on the shore. Joyce and the other friend were walking along the shore, perhaps wearing rubber boots, when Joyce suddenly dropped into a six-foot-deep hole. She went under, and Carl jumped in to rescue her. Both drowned. One of the two friends ran to a nearby house for assistance. Before darkness fell, police divers recovered their bodies. The mother learned of the tragedy from her surviving son, Jerry, when she exited the No. 9 Wilmore bus at Fordham Road and West Boulevard.

It was a time when children were often told by parents to "go out and play". Almost always, nothing of consequence happened other than poison ivy exposure, chigger bites, a fall from a bike, or occasionally a broken bone. According to The *Charlotte Observer* account, Mrs. Burns had warned her children about the pond. This time, when two children were outside on their own, things went horribly wrong. The same pond, unless it is a newer one, is still in the reported location based on satellite imagery. It was then owned by a family living on Watson Drive. They were not home at the time. The pond is long and narrow, indicating a possible use as a borrow pit for "fill dirt" needed for street construction or other use. That might explain an unexpected drop along its shoreline. Whatever its genesis, the excavation filled with water as the area is on the downslope from the ridgeline parallel to the Southern Railway tracks, and a tributary creek appears to run very close by.

I remember my father discussing with "Big Mama" whether I should visit the funeral home as they were called then. One evening, my father took me. It was perhaps a poor decision, although I can understand their rationale. It was too much for me; I internalized my reaction. Joyce Burns was two years ahead of me. I saw her almost every day. It was a brutal beginning to the new year, and it had a lasting impact. I have not swum in a river or lake since, and I never truly enjoyed playing in the ocean at our coast on beach trips.

My father's late afternoon errands might take me to Julian's Laundry at 918 East Morehead. It is now an empty building. In the early fifties, bus drivers and many other occupations required their employees to wear uniforms. My father – and many other bus drivers – looked as if they could report for national guard duty, albeit in different uniforms. My father took pride in his martial appearance – shoes shined, starched shirts, a nicely shaped dress hat. Eisenhower-style jackets were available for cooler weather, especially needed since bus doors often open. His shirts had heavy starch and were folded neatly with a cardboard liner and a band wrapping them, then stacked in a brown paper package. My grandmother would "turn" the shirt's collars and cuffs for my father when they began to fray. Turning them over would prolong the life of a shirt. Drivers had to purchase their company clothing through Duke Power. His dress, like the well-attired guys in film noir movies of the time, made a lasting impression on me.

The bus garage at East Bland and South Blvd was another destination. The building was the former streetcar barn where trolley cars were held up during the night. When the last streetcars ceased operation in 1938, the garage was repurposed for buses. I liked walking among the buses, which were parked end to end in rows on either side of a firewall in the center of the building. It was great stuff and something my friends did not experience. There was an adjacent lot where other buses were parked, and yet another lot next to it. There was a ready room with restrooms and some lockers on the south side of the building. That is where drivers would congregate. I heard a lot of things there, some not suitable for this narrative, but all of which were

Chapter 2 - A Kid of Six, Eight, Ten……

part of life's practical education.

Across the street at 1317 was the Hot Shoppe, a typical diner. It opened early so first shift drivers could have breakfast before sunrise. Across East Bland Street was Lance Packing Company. Yes, that was Lance the cracker folks. Their tractor-trailer trucks would use Bland Street to back into the loading dock. Of course, crackers came in four packs only. Lance had competition – Mitchum and Tucker (M&T) and Swinson Products. Swinson was downtown at 600 South College. They remained there for several decades, frequently releasing the pleasing aroma of fresh baking downtown.

My favorite stop was The Hobby Shop, owned by Jack Shuman, and near Pritchard Memorial Baptist Church, at 1211 South Boulevard It was a repurposed former residence. The front porch had been enclosed with glass, and there were seemingly countless model airplanes hanging in those full-height windows. Sometimes we would stop and go in. My modeling skills were about non-existent at six/eight years, but I was captivated by what might be. Plastic injection-molded kits were new to the hobby market in the early fifties, and were quickly displacing the various types of wooden models. For a while in the 1950s, plastic model companies would send assembled kits in small, printed cardboard dioramas to many stores that stocked their products. Injection-molded plastic kits simply overwhelmed the wooden model kit market beginning in 1952/53, and within two or three years, my friends and I had deserted wooden models. Patience is a rare attribute when one is 10 or 11, so plastic was the clear choice. Their benefit was that a kid could buy a model for about 59 cents, a tube of glue for a dime, and an hour later, he could be flying missions in the neighborhood.

It was in my father's '49 Ford Custom Line, parked in front of The Hobby Shop, that I resolved one of the big conundrums of my childhood. During the Korean War, June 25, 1950 – July 27, 1953, my father listened daily to radio news programs. I heard a lot about "North Korean Gorillas". In fact, it was "guerillas", but I did not know that distinction. My friends and I had many academic discussions on the topic. We could not rationalize how anyone could train gorillas to march, carry rifles, and take orders.

It was on a notable and revelatory afternoon, after a news program about the war, that I posed a question to my father, who explained the difference.

What a relief to know our guys in South Korea did not face 800-pound North Korean gorillas carrying rifles and hand grenades!

Statesville Avenue

The bounds of my adventures sometimes extended beyond the South Blvd/West Boulevard corridors and their adjacent neighborhoods. "Big Mama's" brother, R. A. Carter, owned and lived on acreage at 2108 Statesville Avenue between Woodward and Kohler Avenues. Carter Avenue was a short street directly behind their property. Imagine a farm only a couple of miles from the center of the city. The land was inherited by my great-uncle's wife, Janie Douglas Kimbrell Carter. It was one of the City's best-kept secrets. Tax records show they once sold 27 lots on Douglas Terrace, a street apparently planned but never built.

The old house – from the post-Civil War period – had major framing fastened with pegs, and was constructed at the top of a shallow rise far back from Statesville Avenue. Their property was mostly shielded by trees and shrubs. Thereon were several large crop fields, small farm buildings, a cow, chickens, the requisite number of dogs and cats, grape vines, fruit trees, and about anything I might want to satisfy my quest for adventure. It was a 4.5-acre site. It was the perfect locale for a boy to replicate his diet of "B" western movies and pursue hostiles across the countryside. There was even a field large enough to hit golf balls. My father, "Big Mama", and I would often visit on summer evenings. We always returned home with vegetables from their garden. They had no modern plumbing. There was an outhouse near the barn. The architecture of the well house indicated the homesite was likely one of a wealthy family. Carter and his wife lived in only two rooms: a bedroom, and a kitchen. I wanted so badly to explore elsewhere inside the house, but understood that it was not a question appropriate to pose to them. My favorite memory is gulping down ripe Concord and Catawba grapes from their arbors. They sold the property in 1972 and moved to an acreage off US 601 south of Monroe. Sadly, they each passed away within several years. The hidden farmland and its giant oaks in the shadows of downtown were soon gone. Today, the land is the site of the Double Oaks Family Aquatic Center.

The drive out to Statesville Avenue (sometimes called Statesville Road)

Chapter 2 - A Kid of Six, Eight, Ten......

began heading east on West Boulevard, across the creek bottom land that was Abbott Park - and now the path of Interstate 77 – and to Wilmore School, where we turned left on South Mint Street. Wilmore Elementary was built in 1925 and was effectively the western anchor of the Wilmore area south of the central city. Wilmore and Dilworth defined the south side of the city's corporate limits in 1930. South Mint Street north of Dowd Road was a collection of industrial and supply businesses. Little Hardware at 1332 South Mint was a virtual landmark. We would cross West Morehead, and just ahead on the left was Good Samaritan Hospital – a hospital established in 1891 for "colored" people. It was addressed at 411 West Hill Street and was easily seen across its parking lot from Mint Street. A sign denoted it as the state's first hospital for Negroes. In fact, on July 27, 1911, there was a train collision in Hamlet, east of Charlotte. One train was carrying Black passengers from Durham. Several people were killed and many were injured. Reports from the time indicated that many of the injured had to await treatment until they were transferred via Seaboard Railroad to Charlotte and Good Samaritan. The hospital closed in 1961, and Panther Stadium stands on the site now.

My father would cross over to South Graham Street. We would go under the plate girder bridge that carried Southern Railway passenger trains from the Columbia Division tracks that paralleled College Street to the Southern Station on West Trade. Just past the bridge on the left was The Atlantic Brewing Company, known for Atlantic Ale and Beer, located at 300 South Graham Street. It ceased operating late in the 1950s.

On the northeast corner of West Trade and Graham was the Coddington - later James K. Polk - Building of 1924. The first floor was the Langston – Moore Plymouth - DeSoto dealership. It was known by Langston's first name - Bobo - and it seemed everyone called it Bobo Langston DeSoto. DeSoto was my favorite Chrysler vehicle, and it had a good run as Chrysler's best-looking steed, but sales fell after 1956, in part due to marketing decisions and the 1958 recession. Chrysler ceased production of the mark early in the 1961 model year. Later in my career, I was finally able to see the building's interior. It was an early site-cast concrete structure, the column tops of which flared outward with shear cones where they met the second floor above. The building was used by the State for some years and ultimately wrapped in scaffolding around 2000 due to failing brick cladding that had begun to separate and fall to the sidewalks. It was demolished some years later for new apartment construction.

We would cross West 5th Street, and just ahead on the right at 6th Street was the used car lot for Thomas Cadillac – Olds. The dealership was located at 214 North Church Street and had no space for used vehicles, so their inventory resided at the lot on the southeast corner of Sixth Street and North Graham. A CVS pharmacy occupies the northwest corner of Graham and Sixth today. For decades, that was the site of Carolina Rim and Wheel, one of many well-known auto service businesses in the downtown area. Across the street was Automotive Electric Associates. In later years, their master mechanic, Herman Brown, would service my automobiles. A short distance away was a new motel, the Orvin Motor Court at 307. It was no doubt constructed on busy Graham Street to capture some of the through-town traffic of US 29.

Bethune School was at 601 as there were still many children in the surrounding neighborhood, although that was quickly changing. Its playground was adjacent to busy Graham Street. A mix of single-family homes, apartment buildings, and several service stations held the streetscape going northward. Graham was the western boundary of what we called the Fourth Ward. To my young mind, it seemed past its heyday even in the 1950s. We had a relative, Mrs. Ratcliff, who lived at 624, and I recall we visited her once. We sat on the front porch only a few yards from what was at the time US 29. Since there was no Interstate 85 north/southbound traffic would turn off West Morehead onto Graham at Younce's Gulf (500 West Morehead, now Panther Stadium) or was funneled to Graham via Dalton Avenue from North Tryon to bypass downtown. Even then, my father would complain about the trucks on narrow Graham Street. That helped lead to the eventual decline of the neighborhood. Interstate 85 relieved the traffic issue in September 1958, but it was too late for the neighborhood. The zoning and transportation sensitivities we take for granted today did not prevail then.

We crossed two narrow four-lane railroad bridges, first the Seaboard Airline Railroad, and then over the Southern Railway. Seaboard crossed Southern at grade but out of sight just past the Seaboard bridge, and I could

Chapter 2 - A Kid of Six, Eight, Ten……

never imagine just how that happened. The Interstate Milling complex (now ADM) stood adjacent to the tracks. It was then that Graham changed to Hutchinson Avenue, and Statesville Avenue departed to the left. The Carter farm would be only minutes away!

The Missile Plant

To reach the Carter farm, we drove outbound on Statesville Avenue. About 1953 or so, Sealtest Dairy built an imposing edifice in the fork of Statesville Avenue/Hutchinson Avenue. It was a combination office and processing building. Sealtest, of course, was a big dairy name at the time, along with Foremost, Biltmore, Pet, and Harvey B. Hunter (a local dairy). Just beyond Sealtest was Dalton Avenue, which carried North US 29 from Tryon to Graham Street. The Big Bertha truck stop building is still on the east corner and has been repurposed for offices.

As we traveled north on Statesville Avenue (US 21), we soon crossed the Southern Railway track that served the huge industrial complex, which is known today as Camp North End. The general history of the site - 72 to 80 acres depending on source – has been well documented. It was a former Ford assembly plant, then a US Army Quartermaster Depot, then Douglas Aircraft Company, and later an Eckerd's Drugs warehouse. Less well documented is just what Douglas did in that facility. The Charlotte Area Missile Plant – CAMP – was Charlotte's notable contribution to the Cold War.

Post WWII Europe did not evolve as envisioned as the Soviet Union wrapped an Iron Curtain around Eastern Europe from the Baltic to the Aegean. There was a fear that global tension between the US and Russia might cause hostilities. In such an event, it was plausible the Soviets might execute a nuclear first strike. Among other things the United States constructed an in-depth defense of search radars (DEW line, mid-Canada line, the so-called Texas Towers off northeast coast, and the first generation of AWACS aircraft), jet fighters or interceptors (how the term was corrupted to fighter jets is a mystery), and anti-aircraft missile installations to defend against air attack.

The Department of Defense contracted the former quartermaster depot facility in 1954 to Douglas, whose other plants were on the West Coast, for use as a manufacturing plant for anti-aircraft missiles. Douglas Aircraft Company, along with Lockheed and Boeing, were iconic American industrial aviation giants. Douglas, by 1950, was already into its DC-7 series of passenger airliners. It had built multiple famous military aircraft in WWII and was still producing aircraft for both the Air Force and the Navy.

Douglas created and produced the first effective surface-to-air missile, the Nike Ajax.

The Ajax used a single-stage, solid propellant booster in conjunction with its main stage motor to lift the missile at 1,600 MPH to an altitude of 60,000 feet. The early Ajax missiles were built elsewhere until the Charlotte plant was operational. The Ajax was soon replaced by the nuclear-capable Nike Hercules, which bundled four Ajax boosters that could launch a Hercules on a trajectory that could reach Mach 4+ and up to 90,000 feet – impressive even today. Eventually, some 250 Nike battery sites became operational at one time or another in the US and among our European and Asian allies. By the mid-sixties, Douglas completed production contracts and then continued to make spare parts for a couple of years. The plant almost certainly also produced Honest John tactical missiles used by the US Army.

The plant was tremendously large, and its exterior so relatively undefined that any streetside visual inspection would hardly reveal its purpose. Its entire output was Charlotte's significant contribution to national defense and the protection of our allies abroad. No Nike missiles or any other missiles were installed at any time around Charlotte. The nearest Nike installations were in the Norfolk area. Today, we know the complex as Camp North End.

Heading East–US 74-East Independence Boulevard/Monroe Road

Another traveling adventure would be a trip to Wadesboro and to Morven in Anson County. My father was born in Morven and his mother had lots of relatives and friends there. It was a long trip and would begin on East Seventh Street near the landmark Stanley Super Drugs at Seventh and Caswell Road. There was a City of Charlotte water tower very close to the intersection. We traveled on Pecan until we crossed the Seaboard tracks at the former "East Yard" at which Seaboard stored freight cars. Anything associated with railroading was exciting for me. At the time there was little liability in storing freight cars there. The operational requirement would cease in another twenty years, about the same time unattended freight cars would become an unnecessary risk for railroads.

We would cross the tracks and a short distance away we turned right onto Independence Boulevard that opened in 1949 as a new path for US 74 into the City. There were homes on Independence above street level, so their front lawns terminated against rather tall concrete retaining walls. The street had been cut below the existing grade which might have mitigated road noise. We passed the Chantilly area at Briar Creek Road that was a grade intersection then but now carries over the Independence Freeway. Just ahead on the right was the original Charlotte Coliseum opened in 1955. Apparently, it and the adjacent David A. Ovens Auditorium were considered something of a cultural/arts node for the still new boulevard. Colonel J. Norman Pease relocated the architectural-engineering firm that carried his name from downtown to a site directly across the boulevard from Ovens. Anecdotal history is Colonel Pease sold an adjacent parcel to someone for a use that did not materialize. A bowling alley was built instead – there went the neighborhood as the saying goes. The long story of how Independence became an essential but congested retail arterial strip, the impacts of which were not remedied until the 1990s will be explored in Chapter 4.

Until East Independence was constructed Seventh Street/Monroe Road was the main east-west route of US 74 through Charlotte. Sometimes we would travel that route which entirely suited me since we would cross under the Seaboard plate girder bridge just past the fire department training tower at the Fifth Street intersection. The training tower and former Firemen's Hall are now an event venue. There was a new Kroehler furniture warehouse just past Briar Creek Road at 3412.

When we crossed the present Sharon Amity Road, and as we passed Sharon Memorial Park Cemetery the city faded behind us. Not far ahead was the intersection with Rama Road – an old farm road connecting to Sardis Road. The very large white house, built by the Wallace family, at the corner where Rama intersected Monroe Road still stands today. Jim Hunnicutt, an engineer at J. N. Pease Associates, where I would later work, purchased the home around 1960. When Rama was eventually re-aligned with Idlewild the giant home was moved a short distance. It exists today as a private learning academy.

Ahead was East Mecklenburg High School which opened in 1950. A connector from Independence intersected Monroe Road at that location. Just past the present Thermal Road intersection on the left was a site occupied by Monroe Road Drive-In theater. It did not have the longevity of other drive-ins and closed in the early sixties. The Chasewood Apartments now occupies the site. We would cross under another railroad bridge in an "S" curve near McAlpine Creek. Monroe Road is much wider now, and a newer bridge still carries CSX (Seaboard then) eastward to Matthews. The drive to Matthews was wooded countryside, and it seemed like a long one, and it was.

North Tryon

North Tryon Street within the city's core was a regular beat of mine. While it lacked the class of its reciprocal to the south, North Tryon extended a long way from The Square with a significant diversity of commerce, services, and transportation – it was highway US Highway 29. For those reasons I have bundled it with the other arterial thoroughfares of this chapter. Its first two blocks within the heart of the city are addressed in Chapter 3.

North Tryon Street offered yet another adventure. In June 1955 when my grandmother returned to Florida for a couple of years, I entered a more advanced phase of my childhood adventures. My father began driving the No. 11 North Tryon-East Morehead bus route that summer. I remember he usually was assigned bus 881, a 36 passenger GMC old look style diesel bus. The No. 11 route was a simple out and back. In 1955 the headway was every 20 minutes. North Tryon was a cornucopia of commerce, manufacturing, and transportation.

In summer of 1955 I saw piles being driven for the new Charlotte-Mecklenburg Library at North Tryon and East 6th Street. It was replaced in the early 1990s with another new building which is being replaced in 2025 by yet another structure. I was puzzled by the Hotel William R. Barringer on the southeast corner of Tryon and Ninth Streets. Even then it seemed the Barriger was in the wrong place. Unlike architecture of recent decades, its only concession to the streetscape was the decorative base which was typical of skyscrapers at that time. Many Hollywood stars and notables reportedly

Chapter 2 - A Kid of Six, Eight, Ten......

stayed there at various times. I divined from listening to adults that hotels were on the way out. Its prime years were about two decades. It began to lease office space about 1970 and ended its run in 1975 under another name. The Charlotte Housing Authority maintained occupancy for public housing – Hall House - for many years but all the materials used to create the edifice and the spaces within now reside in a landfill, a casualty of our expanding city's growth. Then as now, across Tryon was the enduring classic First United Methodist Church. The White Tower restaurant was adjacent to the church at 511, where the Plaza area for 525 North Tryon Building is today.

The handsome brick structure at 500 was once a paint store and by 1958 was the Gold Bond Stamps redemption store. For a time, grocery stores, some service stations and other businesses would offer coupon stamps that correlated to the value of consumer purchases – much like gasoline points from supermarkets today. Green stamps were another big stamp name. Consumers would collect, then paste them in booklets. The stamps could then be redeemed for merchandise. It was an early version of customer loyalty rewards. The Guthery Apartment building at 508 still exists today. It was one of numerous locations of the city's "downtown" population. The last remaining eighteenth-century home for some distance on North Tryon was between Ninth and Phifer (now Montford Point). The date of its demise is in question, but the block is owned by Mecklenburg County and offers a canopy of trees in contrast to nearby parking lots and buildings. In an interesting twist, in 1960 the upscale Manger Motor Inn opened at 631 North Tryon. It was known for its Hearth and Embers Restaurant. Its appearance likely hastened the decline of the Barringer Hotel - fodder for a good academic discussion by urban specialists. Its construction did little to change the perception that North Tryon was in decline.

My father's bus would always stop for loading/unloading at 700 North Tryon. Sears (Sears Roebuck) moved in 1949 to 700 North Tryon. Previously the store resided at 304-306 South Tryon. Reportedly the *Charlotte Observer* noted its move was too far from the center city. In retrospect Sears was a presage of how K-Mart, Walmart and other retailers would dim the appeal of uptowns in the 1960s and beyond. The store spanned from Tryon to College Street and its auto shop was across College Street. Most importantly, there was plenty of onsite parking. Sears was known for its famous catalog, for Kenmore appliances, and for Craftsman tools. Children of the fifties likely remember the cutaway washing machine that enabled customers to see the inner working of a washer in action. Each Christmas the toy department would exhibit a Lionel display train layout – an irresistible incentive to visit the store. It offered a restaurant, auto repair garage, and a garden shop. Sears relocated to the new Eastland Mall in the mid -1970s.

Opposite Sears was the First Associate Reform Presbyterian church, now known as the McColl Center. It was heavily damaged by fire and was empty for many years. Across Eleventh Street at 801 Tryon is the building that was once an A&P grocery store, in a style and size that typified A&P stores. Continuing northward we crossed under the Seaboard Airline Railroad. The rail bridge was a heavy concrete structure with multiple tracks and still carries CSX traffic. The Seaboard passenger station was above Tryon Street level, and I had no way to see it as we ducked under the bridge. It was farther north than I wanted to walk from the square – I had the shoe leather but not the time. Seaboard's Charlotte passenger service was provided by its Wilmington to Rutherfordton daily run via its hub in Hamlet - one train a day in each direction by the early 1950s. At East Sixteenth Street, we would go under another massive bridge that carried multiple Southern Railway tracks over Tryon. Usually, I could see some action there as diesels switched the large yard that lay between Tryon and Brevard Streets. Flooding in heavy rains was common at the low point under the bridge. On the corner at Sixteenth Street at 1224 was the Foremost Dairy (a large national dairy) grill and ice cream shop.

Just beyond the Dalton Avenue intersection on the right was Purina Chows. From it at almost any hour wafted a characteristic and most pungent odor of animal feeds. I would hold my breath as my father's bus passed by it. Occupying 1925 North Tryon was Radio station WSOC, far back from Tryon behind a signature long front lawn. A notable architectural structure was located at 2309 North Tryon – The Alamo Plaza Motor Court. It was the first chain of motels in the nation. All Alamo facades featured their signature faux Spanish territorial architecture. The Charlotte Alamo had a face lift in the early 1960s but faded as interstates siphoned away through town traffic.

An eclectic mix of banking, equipment dealers, tire companies, and trucking filled out North Tryon streetscape. We passed Central Motor Lines located at 2600 before the bus reached the end of its line in the gravel lot of an old Amoco service station at 2924. I liked to go into the station and if I were hungry, I might have a Dinner Bell ham and cheese with chocolate milk. The layover at the end of the line was brief so soon it would be time to return to the square and I was always glad as the station was across the street from Speas Vinegar plant at 2921 Tryon. The air was always heavy with the smell of vinegar.

The North 29 Drive-In theater was farther out of town on the left near Craighead Road. Just beyond Sugar Creek Road on the right was the fairgrounds. Once my father took me to the Southern States Fair. It had two entrance structures that were near the present location of the Advance Auto Parts Store. My assessment as a boy of eight was: there were a lot of strange people at the fair. Next home for the fair was Metrolina Fairgrounds off US 21 north of the city.

Wilkinson Boulevard   US29/74 West

What were the destinations for someone on Charlotte's west side for those from other areas of the city? A fish camp at the Catawba River, airport amusement park, Forest Lawn Cemetery/Mausoleum, driving range on Old Dowd Road, restaurants: Ranch House, Staley's Charcoal Steakhouse, to name just a few that come to mind.

The Open Kitchen and The Gondola would make the list for pizza – pizza pie as many of us called it — and Plantation Grill for its all-around menu. Once a big attraction, the racetrack near Wilkinson Blvd and Little Rock Road had long ago closed. Of course, we must add the airport to the list and not just for the purpose of catching a flight. A respectable list of venues.

Then as now the airport was what's happening. Aviation in Charlotte has always been centered on the west side. Eastside activity was minimal - there was Wilgrove Airport off NC24/27 (closed in summer of 2020). At nearby Delta Airbase planes too big to fly out once landed to be salvaged for parts. It was close to what is now WT Harris Boulevard Otherwise, aviation activities resided on the west side.

Cannon Airport was likely a direct outcome of WWI Camp Greene. It was the point of service for what little commercial air traffic Charlotte had after WWI and was known as the Charlotte Airport. It was parallel to what became Ashley Road. Freedom Mall with its Richway store would later occupy the site. Its buildings have since been repurposed for County offices. When playing in the woods surrounding the field, my friends Jack Washam, Craig Pergerson, Richard Harris and David Atwood would sometimes discover a former building foundation that was part of Camp Greene. "Dead Man's Cave" was reputed to have been just off Greene Street between Royston Road and Freedom Drive.

When the United States entered WWI, the Army looked for training camps in locations with supposedly good weather. Charlotte's boosters worked hard to secure a camp for Charlotte. Named for Revolutionary War commander Nathaniel Greene, a new camp was hastily constructed in the general area from the Thrift Road/West Morehead intersection westward and by Thrift/Tuckasegee Roads to about where I-85 presently exists, and thence following Ashley Road, or Greene Boulevard as it was known in the 1930s, then to Wilkinson Boulevard The camp perimeter crossed over Wilkinson Blvd to the Southern Railway tracks. The name Remount Road is likely derived from a calvary remount station near the tracks (horses were still part of the Army then). References to streets named for the camp may be spelled "Green" or "Greene". A sampling of documents and maps will show both spellings.

A photo from the time shows Cannon Airport was visited in the early thirties by Amelia Earhart. There were no doubt mail flights into Cannon, keeping in mind that the preponderance of mail traveled by train. My father would drive my grandfather and me to Cannon and park on the shoulder of what was once known as Greene Blvd (Ashley Road). One of four runways – all were sod - was very close to the property fence. We would watch mostly Piper Cubs of various types taxi out, take off and land. The weekends were the best times to catch the action. There was no tower on site so pilots would check the windsock, and if landing get into the pattern and land. That is where I learned about downwind leg, base leg, and final approach.

I did not know at the time, but the site was likely a sentimental experience for my father. He was a civilian pilot prior to WWII and engaged to my mother when he made his last flight from Cannon. His carefully maintained flight log entry for his final takeoff as a civilian is 10:30 a.m., Sunday December 7, 1941. Within 24 hours he had volunteered for the US Army Air Corps (later Army Air Forces).

To Douglas Airport

For a visit to the airport one drove either Wilkinson Blvd or West Boulevard In the fifties the airport was "in the country". Wilkinson was US 29/74, a busy four lane and commercially developed highway that was built in the 1920s. It was the route to the airport, to the textile region around Gastonia, Kings Mountain, Atlanta, and to Asheville (US 29 and US 74 split as they still do west of Gastonia).

Before the big flood of 1916 which took out the original bridge over the Catawba, Dowd Road was the route westward. Dowd began at its intersection with South Mint Street and mostly paralleled the Southern Railway tracks to the river. Wilkinson followed Dowd Road, but "Old" Dowd diverted somewhat to the south just beyond Mulberry Church Road. Segments of it exist today and it returns to Wilkinson opposite the Amazon facility just east of the river. In the fifties Wilkinson was a four-lane undivided highway without turn lanes. The road shoulders were dirt/gravel and often used for parking at various establishments. Turn lanes with signals were not common in the 1950s. Adults often discussed automobile accidents on Wilkinson. Our home was midway between Wilkinson and West Boulevard, and indeed, we could hear more than the usual number of sirens on weekends and evenings.

Dowd Road intersected Wilkinson Blvd at its juncture with West Morehead. The Western part of Independence Blvd replaced Dowd and was completed by 1957. There were many Wilkinson landmarks that survived for decades – some buildings are still extant. In the small triangle between former Dowd Road and West Morehead was Lindy's Grill, later to be The Gondola. As were most Italian restaurants, it was Greek owned - Steve and Gus Economos. The building is now a smoke shop. Across Morehead was The Plantation. It was a classic 40s/50s restaurant. There was a canopy for curb service at its rear, also a counter for takeout. As late as 1959 one could have a quarter fried chicken dinner with slaw, roll and fries for $0.59. The

Plantation was noted for its blue-ribbon small steak and hamburger steaks. It was owned by Joe Edwards whose daughter was a classmate of mine. It was managed by Pergy Pergerson, father of a dear friend and classmate Craig. Unfortunately, the only known image is imprinted on match book covers. Clark's Esso station was next door on the corner of Wilkinson and Berryhill Road. Both are gone and a new pet grooming business occupies the site.

Just past Berryhill on the right was a fine period example of a post WWII commercial center: Colonial Supermarket at 2412, Kiser Hardware 2408, and Kiser Drugs 2400. Offices for a dentist and a doctor were located above the pharmacy. Kiser's daughter was a classmate of mine. In the late fifties the drug store was enlarged to be more competitive with larger pharmacies. The land was too valuable for a grocery store so in the early 1960s the center was demolished. A new Howard Johnson motel/restaurant was constructed there, after which the earlier HJ restaurant across the street at 2401, with its signature orange terra cotta tile roof, was demolished. The site is now apartments.

Staley's Charcoal Steaks and Catalina Motel – upscale for the time – went up in the mid/late fifties across from Kiser's center at Berryhill and Wilkinson. A few yards away to the west was the Town and Country Drive-In restaurant. The Town and Country was one of the "drive throughs" for those of us cruising in the sixties. Unlike other locations, T & C sold beer. I did not drink but my friend James Sanders did so we would sometimes stop there for a while. New apartment buildings frame both sides of the boulevard now.

The brick building that housed General Dyestuffs, at 2459 is still there but with multiple tenants. It is the architectural class of the strip. The Toddle House and Shell service station, that occupied the remaining lots moving toward Remount Road, are now part of an auto sales dealer. Across Wilkinson, Monument Avenue still intersects very close to Remount Road. Its name derived from a monument to WWI Camp Greene. The historic Dowd House, which was the headquarters building of the camp graces the street and faces Arty Avenue – purportedly short for "artillery". The church near the monument was once known as Camp Green Presbyterian Church. Pneumafil Company had a large plant on the northwest corner of Remount Road at 2500 Wilkinson. It is now the site of Graybar.

Chapter 2 - A Kid of Six, Eight, Ten......

Continuing westward, the building that housed Stratford Furniture at 2541 (later Goings-Stratford) is still opposite the Greene Street intersection. Parker Animal Hospital at 2640 is now adjacent to a new Fire Station, which is next to Dairy Queen, now in its ninth decade. Bar B Que King, which certainly looks unchanged and dates to 1960 (some sources state 1959), is just beyond the animal hospital at Weyland Avenue. BBQK was my cruising hangout in the sixties. Southern Engineering, a westside landmark and known as Little Pittsburgh, was a structural steel fabricator at 3015 Wilkinson on the southeast corner of Ashley Road and Wilkinson. A Quick Trip gas station is there today.

During the daytime one could feast at Bar-B-Que King and watch steel structural shapes being fabricated at Little Pittsburgh directly across from BBQK. Opposite a short side street was and still is the County School Bus maintenance garage. The site of the current Walmart was an open space of red clay soil. There were abandoned vehicles there, including two Army DUKWs (ducks) which always fascinated me. In the early 2000s Walmart built on the site which in the late 1960s Woolworth had constructed a large Woolco store – its competitor for K-Mart. All 282 Woolco stores were closed in 1982.

Moving a little farther westward was the Discount House, 2836, and Park N Shop, 2938. Both were on the right just past the present CVS. The Discount House was something of an early crossover combo of Walmart and Dollar General. Not sophisticated but entirely useful.

Park-N-Shop is a story of its own. It was a private supermarket. Charles Reid was its creator and owner. His daughter was a classmate. Wilkinson was its only location until a second store was built on North Tryon Street at the former fairgrounds site. Later a third was constructed on South Boulevard, another on East Independence Boulevard It was open until midnight to serve those who worked late shifts. In those days shoppers would put their various vegetables and produce in paper pokes (bags) and then have them weighed. All supermarkets had weighing stations. A staffer would weigh the bag and then mark a price on it – a long way from UPC Codes. For many years the Hilton sisters, two cojoined twins, stood back-to-back where they were connected and weighed produce during the day shift at Park-N-Shop. The *Charlotte Observer* did a special feature following their deaths.

Park-N-Shop was known for its "field wagons" that were tractor-trailer trucks serving only Reid's stores, going directly to sources for fruits and vegetables, bypassing distributors and thereby promoting lower prices. Park N Shop was perhaps a predecessor of Walmart Grocery and Aldi in a large conventional supermarket format.

Traveling Wilkinson, we would pass many businesses until 4110 - South 29 Drive-In Theater. The southeast corner at Morris Field Drive is almost unchanged, same motel with a different name that was there in the fifties. On the southwest corner of Wilkinson and Morris Field Drive was a new parts distribution building constructed by Ford in the early fifties at 4301. The site today has a new building housing Mecklenburg EMS. Nearby at 4615 is an inauspicious, small brick building, which once housed the DMV driver license office and is next to today's Coyote's Joes. The little structure where egos were challenged, and honors were placed on the line now houses an insurance company office. Once upon a time everyone in my high school took their drivers' exam there. Incredibly, one member of my high school class had an accident during a driving test!

Across Wilkinson was an establishment that had an interesting past but did not last long. It was the Star Castle Drive-In Restaurant. It featured a glass windowed second floor tower where its DJ sat and played popular music records for the patrons who enjoyed curbside dining in their automobiles. Nearby the original alignment of Mulberry Church Road has been abandoned, and Mulberry now connects opposite present Boyer Street - once a part of Dowd Road. The driving range is gone. The stucco building that once was the El Morocco supper club is still there in the little triangle between Boyer and Wilkinson. The word around school was that strippers occasionally performed there – wild stuff for the 1950s. The northwest corner of Harlee Avenue and Wilkinson was the site of another well-known restaurant – The Ranch House, which was famous for its hot shrimp cocktail sauce. It survived to the 21st century. Even in 2000, its interior looked like 1956. Its menus were printed on varnished wood. On April 27, 1963, after leaving our prom, my girlfriend and I went to the Ranch House for steaks at 11:00 p.m. in the evening. My stomach must have been of cast iron then.

A short distance away on the left, in an area now rendered unrecognizable by airport construction, was another landmark eatery, Copal's Grill. The

Chapter 2 - A Kid of Six, Eight, Ten......

Copal Motor Court offered 15 modern rooms with both private and connecting baths! Suttle's Pool and Swim Club resided in the bottomland on the right just beyond present I-485. It was a private pool. The pool is gone but the lay of the land looks the same. I-485 now crosses US 29/74 at the precise location of the first Holiday Inn motel in Charlotte, on the south side of the roadway. Opened in late 1957, it had 60 rooms, a pool, restaurant and 24-hour telephone service!

The only reason for my family to venture this far out on Wilkinson Boulevard was River View Inn Fish Camp, at the end of a short stub road just to the right of the Catawba River Bridge.

Turns out in later years River View employed a gentleman with a real wooden leg. Always dressed as Captain Windy, he greeted restaurant guests. The Catawba River was the Mecklenburg County line and the Catawba River Bridge, narrow but wide by pre-war standards, is still one of only three highway bridges (I-85, US 29/74, and NC 27) crossing directly into Gaston County.

Wilkinson was the primary route to Douglas Municipal Airport. Before the new terminal went into operation in 1954/1955 direct access to the terminal was via Morris Field Drive from Wilkinson. An alternative to the terminal area was via Harlee Avenue, which intersected Wilkinson Boulevard directly opposite the Ranch House restaurant. The airport amusement park was on the corner at 5525 where an industrial building resides today. It was a full-time amusement park with a variety of rides and animals and opened on St. Patrick's Day 1951. One Sunday afternoon I visited with my grandparents and my aunt and uncle (my typical transportation service). My grandmother cautioned my grandfather, "Daddy, don't get too close," as he approached a Llama in a pen. In a validation of the posted warning the animal promptly spat on him. Another lesson for me – always heed my grandmother's words.

Harlee then crossed a bridge over the Southern Railway tracks where it made a sharp 90-degree curve to the left and continued through undulating small hills covered in kudzu to Morris Field Drive, basically the route of Minuteman Lane today.

At the sharp curve was also a paved road to the right accessing an aircraft repair/salvage outfit where we could observe worn out airplanes stripped for their parts. Directly in front of the sharp curve was a large gravel parking area, higher than the runway and taxiways. Locals would go to watch planes. At night the parking area doubled as a lovers' lane. It was a safe, populated location, and local police were not intrusive (as I learned in later years). But in earlier years we would leave the site at dusk, I assumed those in the remaining vehicles were still watching planes.

Central Avenue NC 24/27

Charlotte was clearly not considered a big city during those days. But to those of us on foot it could seem quite large. Central began a mile from the Square. Beyond Morningside I did not know just where Central went. I knew of Morningside Drive because it was a bus route destination. Central and The Plaza was a commercial hub then just as today. The Plaza Theatre at 1610 had a few times been a destination and then only with my father. The Plaza was well known for its former streetcar tracks that were ultimately replaced by a wide median. I knew Charlotte Country Club was out there somewhere, and I knew of Commonwealth Avenue. My first visit to Central Avenue on my own was attributable to our new TV.

In early 1959 my father's mother, Big Mama, purchased a 21-inch Westinghouse black and white TV for our duplex home. It was a big deal. It was not a console but mounted on a base with a faux grill behind which I would one day mount my stereo speakers. We used a rabbit ears antenna which all but ensured frequent airplane interference. However, I was finally able to join Monday morning discussions at school about what happened on Maverick and Paladin, among other TV hits of the era. She made the purchase from her nephew who owned Carters of Charlotte Furniture at 2403 Central. It was a $269 expenditure paid via installments – very common at the time. Once a month following the arrival and cashing of her Social Security check, I rode downtown carrying $20. At the Square I transferred to the No 10 Midwood bus. A little way beyond Veterans Park I would pull the cord and disembark from the bus at the correct stop. I would then cross the street and make a payment while the bus ran a loop on Club Road. Stepping out to the curb, I would ride the same bus back downtown.

I never quite found what was "central" about Central Avenue. Perhaps it was a marketing strategy. For the early part of the twentieth century, it was

Chapter 2 - A Kid of Six, Eight, Ten……

a prestigious address. I recall many impressive residences, notwithstanding they appeared to have seen more prosperous times. The Central Avenue corridor was in the northern part of the Elizabeth neighborhood that was heavily impacted by Independence Boulevard. There was a Colonial Store supermarket at the Central and Louise Avenue intersection. The building later found different uses including a meeting venue. The vestiges of the early twentieth century have been swept away by massive apartments and various new construction projects. Land use planning was not in my vocabulary then. Never heard of it in fact. But even at my age I sensed that there were buildings that simply seemed out of place. The "neighborhood movement" of the seventies and beyond had not arrived and my recollection is that citizens and homeowners just accepted what was approved or allowed by City government.

Pet Dairy occupied 1111 Central. It appeared to be a distribution warehouse. There may have been a dairy bar there. Across Hawthorne Lane near the corner was the Central Avenue Methodist Church and more houses. Just ahead was Charlotte Casket Company – 1317- and which was served by the Seaboard RR (CSX) which crossed Central as it still does today. On the left 1327 was the home of Patsy Maner, later Patsy McKinsey, former City Councilperson, County Commissioner, and Mayor. Hard to believe today but Patsy rode a bus downtown and back – by herself — to her piano lessons when she was in the third grade!

In the late 1950s Central Square Shopping Center was constructed just beyond the railroad tracks on the right and across Central from Patsy's home. The center was anchored by the city's most numerous supermarkets, A & P. The area is now under redevelopment. Of note, and years beyond our journey's time frame, the popular Purple Penguin nightspot of the late sixties was at the corner of Pecan and Central. 1517 Central was the location of a well-known suburban clothing store, Sherman's Ltd. Family Dollar occupied 1510 Central. The next couple of blocks were like West Park Avenue with multiple retail services and of course the Plaza Theater. Over the decade there was a considerable turnover of tenants. Plaza Hardware and Hahn Bakery were two of the longer-lived stores. The first Harris Supermarket, now Harris-Teeter, was at the corner of Central and The Plaza. Midwood Elementary was at 1817 Central, and for my journeys it was on past Midwood School and in only a couple of minutes until another TV installment would be history.

Chapter Notes

A&P: The Great Atlantic and Pacific Tea Company, established in 1859, was once the nation's largest retail grocery store chain. Its decline in the Charlotte market began in the 1960s when it began to lose market share to Harris Teeter. Colonial Stores was another supermarket chain that was prominent in Charlotte. Its stores later became known as Big Star before they were all closed or sold to competitors in the 1980s. Winn-Dixie was another large chain that held on but withdrew from Charlotte in the 1990s.

Charlotte History A Mile Wide….: Comments by Dr. Dan Morrill, UNC-C and Chair of Charlotte Mecklenburg Historic Properties Foundation. Bank of America, and partners Corporate Workplace team luncheon 2002.

Southern Railway Dieselization: Railroads rapidly dieselized following WWII. Diesel locomotives, especially switchers, began entering service in the 1920s but by the 1930s were hauling some premier trains. Alco, Baldwin, and GM were the primary manufacturers. General Motors Electro-Motive Division offered their prototype four-unit freight diesel locomotive set in 1939. Each unit was rated at 1,350 HP. Diesels needed only diesel fuel and a crew and were synced together to operate as a single unit. Neither coal nor water (except water for passenger service steam generators) was required. Steam locomotives required heavy shop time and frequent stops for fuel and water. Diesels had electric traction motors on each driving axle, powered by a primary generator, and offered their maximum tractive effort from starting speed. After WWII the economics of diesel operation overtook the staunchest steam advocate railroads and by 1960 mainline steam power in regular service was all but gone. Southern Railway was the first Class 1 railroad to become all diesel in 1953.

Soviet Threat: The Soviets exploded an atomic bomb in 1949, in the early stages of the Cold War, and in 1950 the Korean War began. As it turned out, in WWII several US B-29s landed in Russian territory with battle damage incurred over Japan. The Soviets never returned the aircraft. Tupolev reversed engineered the aircraft, building quite a few almost exact copies known as the TU-4. The Soviet Union then had a bomber that could, on a one-way mission, reach the continental US carrying an atomic weapon.

The United States adopted a strategy of Mutual Assured Destruction (MAD) to ensure destruction of the Soviet Union regardless of level of attack on the US. Before ICBMs (intercontinental ballistic missiles) and the first Polaris nuclear submarines became operational in the early sixties, more advanced jet bombers were the primary delivery system. Missiles gave the US a "Triad" of land-based missiles, submarine launched missiles and land-based bombers. The strategy was that two of the three legs of the "triad" could be lost and there would still be enough firepower to destroy the Soviet Union. The US had three lines of radar stations across Canada, three "Texas Tower" platforms off the northeast US coast, and airborne radar surveillance aircraft to detect a Soviet attack. Douglas "Nike" missiles, both the Ajax and the Hercules models were the primary ground-based defense for selected US cities while the US Air Force Air Defense Command has a massive array of dedicated jet fighters to engage hostile aircraft attempting to penetrate to US targets.

GMC Old Look: General Motors Coach was a division of General Motors Corporation. It was the nation's largest motor coach builder for decades. The so-called "old looks" were its primary model, available in various lengths and seating capacities, from 1940 through 1958 when the streamline "new looks" replaced it. It is an iconic American industrial design. Some "old looks" in a very short model for smaller municipalities were manufactured until 1968.

Father's Flight Log: Civilian pilots were required to maintain flight logs in which they recorded each flight, the aircraft type and serial number, and total time of flight. My father had qualified "solo" and flew out of Cannon Airport and rented J-3 Piper Cubs for most flights. They were noted as "local" which meant simply flying around Mecklenburg and the surrounding area. Almost 20,000 J-3s were manufactured, some are still airworthy.

Three Highway Bridges: Highway NC 49 crossed into York County South Carolina via the Buster Boyd Bridge that was named for a notable Mecklenburg citizen. NC 49 was carried out of the city by South Tryon Street until it became York Road. Like many bridges constructed in the early twentieth century, Buster Boyd was very narrow and replaced in the early sixties with a modern two-lane bridge. A third dual bridge has since replaced the second structure.

Neighborhood Movement: The post WWII years was a period of increased focus on urban planning and zoning issues. Charlotte's government was historically led by individuals from the more affluent east side part of the city. By the 1970s growth, traffic and zoning began to conflict with expectations from citizens. The national activism of the 1960s eventually rolled down to the municipal level and helped establish a mindset that local governments must be more accountable to citizens on issues of quality of life. Charlotte City Council went to a combination district/at-large composition in the late 1970s. Mecklenburg County Commission soon followed. "Neighborhood movement" became the operative phrase for more grass roots citizen participation. Airport noise was a big motivating issue on the westside. In the faster growing areas, there was great resistance to commercial development and higher density housing. The route selection for the southern section of the outer belt road, now I-485, found some neighborhoods joining with developers to oppose other neighborhoods that aligned with the City Council preferred route. In December 1990 the City Council adopted an open meetings ordinance stronger than the state statute. It was a significant accomplishment for a coalition of neighborhoods. Changing demographics, declining interest in governance, changing attitudes toward land use/density and environmental awareness among other things have reduced the presence and effectiveness of neighborhood political power.

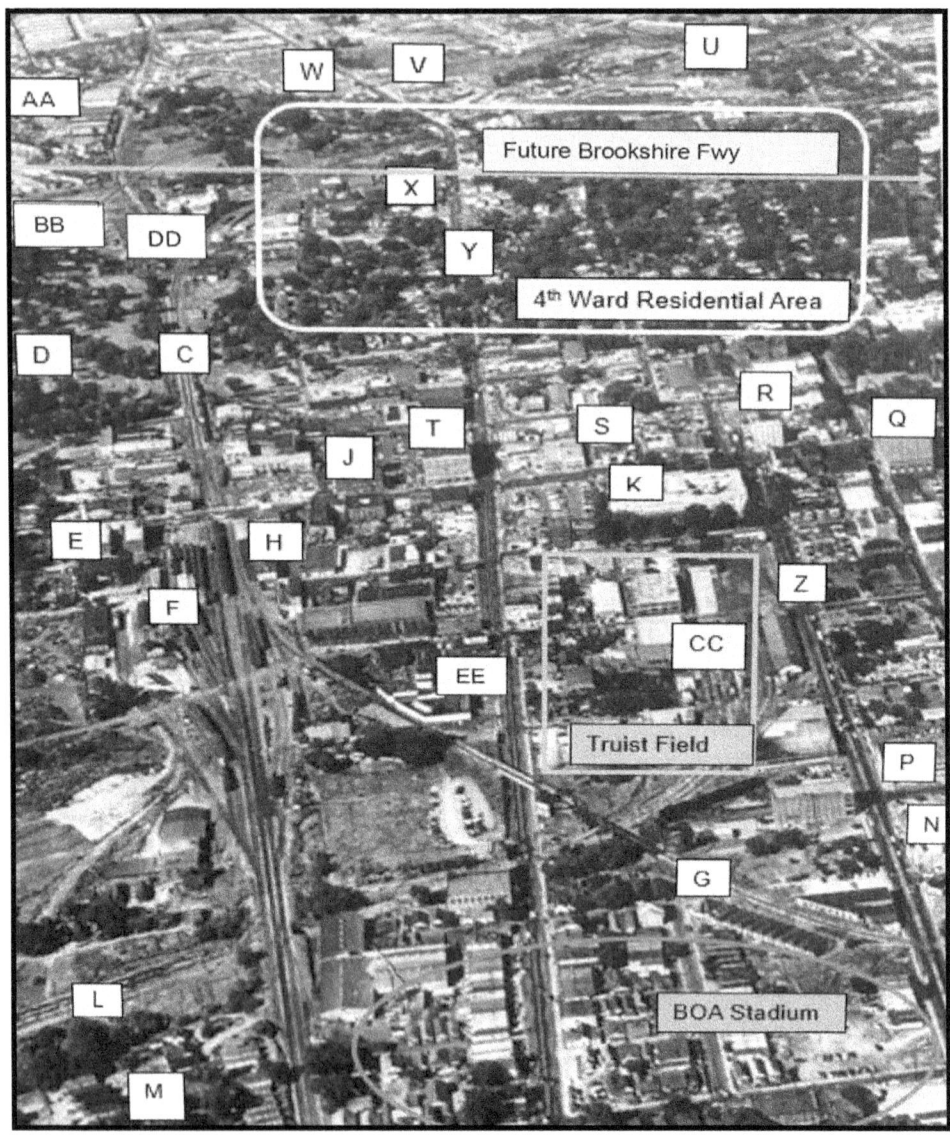

Graham Street Corridor.
Mid-late 1950s. A remarkably well detailed aerial found at a hobby show was taken directly above Good Samaritan Hospital/Graham Street looking north. The Southern Dairy (Sealtest) Building is extant, and Swift and Company on South Mint Street appears to be active which dates the photo between 1953 and late 1950s. Photo: Author's Collection.

Legend

A Good Samaritan Hospital same location as BOA Stadium
B West Hill Street same location as BOA Stadium
C Southern Railway Washington-Atlanta-New Orleans mainline.
D Emwood/Pinewood Cemeteries
E Southern Railway Administration Buildings
F Southern Railway passenger coach yard.
G Southern Railway cutoff for passenger trains to reach Depot from Columbia Division line.
H Southern Railway Depot, presently Greyhound Station, future CATS intermodal facility
J Mecklenburg Hotel
K Federal Courthouse/U S Post Office (Now Charles R. Jonas Federal Courthouse)
L P&N Railway tracks to Mint Street Yard
M Residential area
N Swift and Company Meats
P Mill Power Supply Building
Q Hotel Charlotte
R Builders Building (Peace Building)
S Union bus Terminal
T Coddington Building (Later James K. Polk Building)
U Dalton Avenue (Carried US 29 traffic to North Graham Street)
V Big Bertha Truck Service (Still extant and repurposed)
W Southern Dairy (Sealtest Milk and Ice Cream)
X Bethune School
Y Graham Street – Route to the Carter Farm
Z South Mint Street
AA Douglas Aircraft Company (Nike Missile Plant)
BB Southern Railway Mooresville Line and Statesville Avenue
CC P&N Railway Mint Street Yard and Freight Depot
DD Interstate Milling (now ADM)
EE Atlantic Beer and Ale

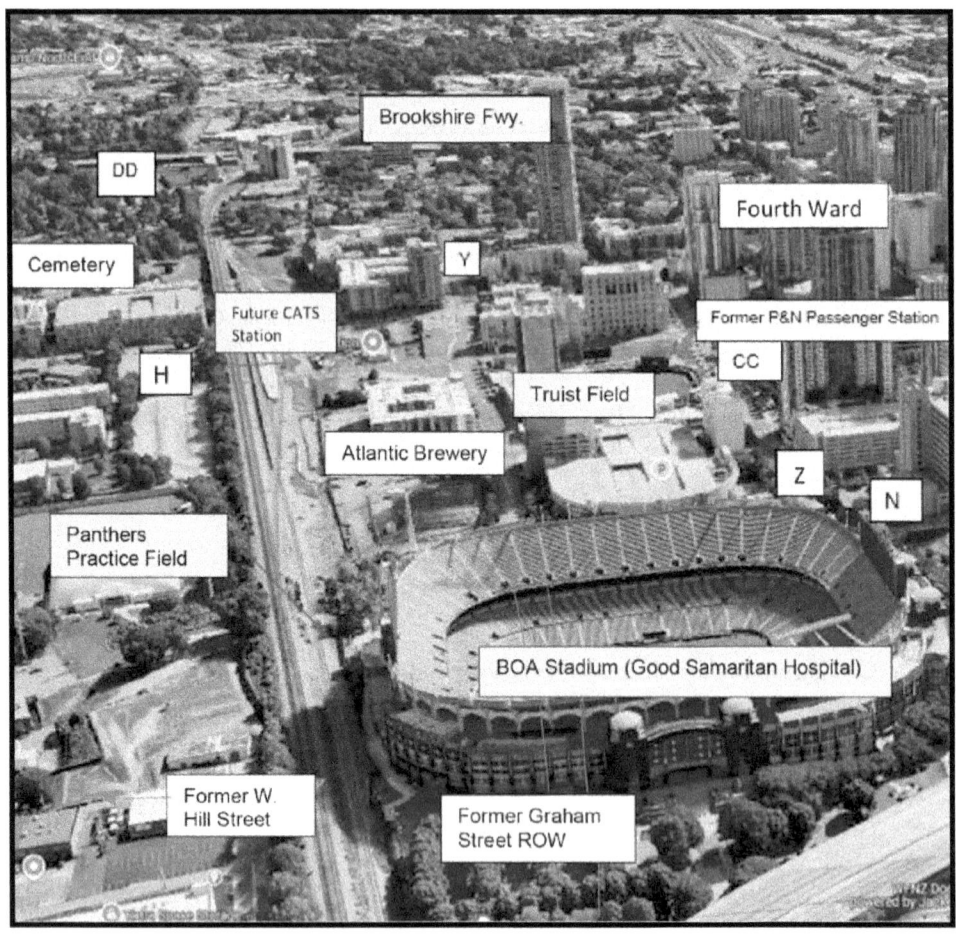

Contemporary Graham Street Corridor.
  Sixty-five plus years later the Norfolk Southern (Southern Railway) main line is still in place, as is ADM (former Interstate Milling Co.). Camp North End (former Douglas Aircraft) is visible in the extreme upper left. Google photo.

North Graham Street. A much wider North Graham Street bridge over Norfolk Southern defines my former pathway to the Carter farm. The significance here: not one of the few buildings that could have been seen in the 1950s is visible today – all are visually obscured by a solid line of new towers. Photo: Author's collection.

West Morehead/Wilkinson/Independence Blvd.

Taken with my Brownie Hawkeye at the city bus stop in front of Clark's Esso Service Station, corner of Berryhill Road and Wilkinson, the 1955/56 Pontiac and one other auto have entered Wilkinson from the end of West Morehead Street. The structure with the tower directly behind the Pontiac is still extant. Several trucking lines and a Putt Putt Golf Course populated the south side of West Independence Blvd seen in the distance. I often rode the No 2 Green Street bus to Ashley Park Elementary School through the fifth and sixth grades. The high angle of the sun at 8:00 AM and the foliage on the trees in front of the building suggest the time was late spring. This photo (May 1957) confirms that West Independence Blvd. was completed to Wilkinson Blvd. by 1957 and possibly late 1956. Photo: Author's collection.

Contemporary Beginning of Wilkinson Blvd.
The Aramark Company building now has a portico and has been expanded but is still defined by the "tower". I was standing at the "star" when I took the previous photo. Before the completion of West Independence, a two-lane Dowd Road connected with Morehead and Wilkinson was constructed in 1926. This area was once part of Camp Green in WWI. Google photo.

BAR-B-Q KING 2900 Wilkinson Blvd.
The sign is original; the establishment essentially changed little from 1960. For Harding and West Mecklenburg students "The King" was a base of operations, their west side anchor. Photo: Author's Collection.

General Dyestuff Corporation 2459 Wilkinson Blvd.
The class of Wilkinson Blvd. This building provided architectural character in the 1950s and is still doing so in the 2020s. An example of repurposing a post WWII classic. It is one of the few remaining Wilkinson Blvd. structures from the 1950s. Google photo.

Dilworth Straight Ahead. South Boulevard looking south at Bland Street. Lance Packing Company (cheese crackers) plant is just out of sight on the right. The former streetcar barn then serving Duke Power Company buses is on the right. Unlike today, only a single four-sided traffic signal controls this intersection and there are no turn lanes. The next traffic signal will be Park Avenue where many businesses that supported the Dilworth and surrounding area's population were located. This photo is dated 1948 although two 1949 Fords are present. The brick structure beyond the bus garage is a Duke Power generating plant that used syngas made in a coal gasification process. The facility may have no longer been active when the photo was taken. Photo: Robinson Spangler Carolina Room, Public Library of Charlotte- Mecklenburg County.

Chapter 3
Adventures Streetside: Downtown and Elsewhere

The Square – Downtown

References to Charlotte's center city were once phrased as "Downtown". The term began to change in the 1970s/1980s to "Uptown" and was soon joined by the phrase "Midtown," which was applied to the Kings Drive area. Likewise, for "South End" along South Boulevard, and NoDa for North Davidson Street. Presumably, "Uptown" was thought to convey sophistication, character, quality, and/or other positive attributes. Why either term was/is used is perhaps more than an academic discussion. Charlotte began at the crossing of two trading paths. In that era, trails (and later roads built thereon), where possible, followed ridge lines or high ground.

To the west of The Square, the term applied to the crossing of Trade and Tryon Streets, lies the Irwin Creek basin, which parallels I-77. To the east runs Little Sugar Creek, which flows roughly north to south about one mile from the Square. Tryon Street follows the ridge line between the two basins, and its local high point in elevation is the Square. From West Blvd northward and from 16th Street southward, almost any movement on Tryon toward the Square is uphill. Trade Street did not follow a ridge line. However, from Irwin Creek or Little Sugar Creek to the Square, it is uphill all the way. The fact is, both terms are still in use as downtown did not depart from our lexicon. This chapter will focus on the center city, and it will be known as "Downtown", the center of which was the "Square".

By Myself in The Big City

It just might be that twenty-first-century parents will have some difficulty accepting that many of my peers and I were allowed to journey downtown by ourselves or with friends when we were 10 years old. I saw lots of guys, including some of my friends, alone downtown, but the girls I saw were always in groups. Girls might have held part-time jobs at Ivey's or Belk, or elsewhere downtown when they were 16 and would ride city buses after school hours or on Saturdays. I might spend most of a Saturday downtown, and neither my grandparents (my mother's mother, Annie, and her husband Pa Pa) nor my father knew precisely where I was at any given time. They knew only that I was downtown. My grandsons once used a Marco Polo App so their parents could know where they were in the neighborhood. Today, we rely on Find My App so we might know where the entire family is.

Knowing how protective I was with our daughter and later our grandsons, I wondered how my father must have felt when he returned his bus to the Square, knowing I was somewhere within a couple of blocks. Among my friends, I was not alone in experiencing new adventures. My schoolmate Leroy Holden rode a city bus from his home in the Tuckasegee/Freedom Drive area to downtown, transferred, and rode to his father's grocery store on Baldwin Avenue, where he worked until closing. Like me, Leroy often spent summer days downtown entirely on his own. Another classmate, Bill Jenkins, walked several miles – each way – to visit his girlfriend.

So just what would a ten-year-old boy do alone in a busy downtown? Firstly, things are contextual to that time. I felt no anxiety, no uniqueness at being on my own. It may not have been entirely common, but I received no unusual attention from adults. Believe it or not, I usually had an itinerary! Saturdays within the school year were subject to a rigorous schedule to pack as much into the day as possible. Summer days were more leisurely. For instance, there was more time to see a movie at the Center theater, which required transferring to another bus route.

During the school year, Saturday would begin with lots of cereal at about 8:00 a.m. I would clean up our duplex and head for the bus stop at 9:10 a.m. It was four blocks away, and my target was to arrive at 9:20 a.m. as the No. 2 Green Street bus left the end of its line at 20 and 50 minutes after each hour. About 9:29 a.m., I would see the bus appear on Wilkinson for its turn onto West Morehead. In the wintertime, it was indeed a relief as there was no shelter at the power pole, which defined the bus stop where Morton Street intersected West Morehead.

Down the hill past WBTV, it offered one of the best views of Charlotte as the center city appeared lofted high into the sky. The white Southern Radio building at 1625 West Morehead, with its full glass front, showcased the latest products from RCA – at the time a premier name in radio/television.

Chapter 3 - Adventures Streetside: Downtown and Elsewhere

Up the hill from Stewart Creek at 1431 was the Grinnell Co. building. It is still there, housing another occupancy. We then drifted past the Coca-Cola plant at West Morehead/Summit Avenue. Through its large windows, I would always see bottles of Coke moving on a conveyor. We would soon turn left onto Cedar Street, and I could have a look at the P&N Railway yard. Sometimes I would see a loaded hopper car being unloaded at F&R Coal & Oil at 624 South Cedar. After turning onto West Trade, we rumbled over the Southern Railway Washington – Atlanta mainline tracks at the vintage Southern Depot, where the Greyhound station is today. The bus would usually arrive at the Square about 9:40 a.m. I would exit in front of Richards Jewelers, which faced the Square from its southwest corner.

The Tryon Theater – 117 South Tryon - opened about 9:50 a.m., so my timing was impeccable. The Tryon's Saturday fare was always a triple feature, with multiple cartoons and sometimes a Three Stooges short as they were called. The Tryon seldom had a newsreel. At 10:00 a.m., over three hours of nonstop adventure would begin. There was always a combo of westerns, a war or military film, and either a comedy or horror movie. The Carolina or Imperial theaters were also always in play. The Charlotte Theater was a little lower scale, but Abbott and Costello or Randolph Scott would easily draw me in.

If Tryon's first movie was good, I might stay for a second showing. By then, it would be about 2:30 p.m in the afternoon. It was then time to reconnoiter the "stores" for the latest model kits. My first stop would be at the Square, where the S.H. Kress façade was a landmark at 101 South Tryon. In fact, Kress had an architectural group that designed its buildings.

I was and still am an avid model builder and model railroader. Johney's Hobby House at 210 South Church Street was also a favorite destination. Johney's was heavy in Lionel trains, which meant heavy cash was required on my part. A $10.95 passenger car was simply out of my range, so I mostly only looked and did not buy. I swam in the sea of plastic model airplanes that flooded the market in the fifties. Kress and Woolworth fit my budget. It was only later in life that I could indulge my railroad empire aspirations.

Johney's may have had the longest lineage of any multiple-location business. The Charlotte Hobby Center at 131 West Fourth Street was around in the late 1940s and owned by John Vogler. Around 1955, it moved to 230 South Church and became Johney's Hobby House soon afterwards. It was a full-service hobby shop. About 1959, Johney's moved to 806 South Kings Drive, now part of a greenway, placing it closer to the better financially resourced areas of the city. The slowly declining train market and parking considerations downtown likely forced the move.

It became a standalone location, limiting my visits to coincide with movies at the Center Theater nearby on East Morehead. About 1970, Johney's relocated to a building in the fork of East Third and Fourth Streets, a location that later initially occupied by Republic Bank and today by Truist Bank. By 1972, the shop had moved to Central Avenue in the vicinity of Piedmont Street. Johney's made it twenty-five or more years in five locations. The last model I purchased there is still in its box, a collector's item now.

Streetside – Tryon and Trade Streets

Tanner's was located at 123 South Tryon Street (for a few years also at 307 North Tryon). They had a venue rental room upstairs, and I suspect they also did private catering. They had a contemporary style stand-up counter and a wall-mounted counter, also. They would dump boxes of oranges into one of their window fronts – the one on the right side of the door. A lady could often be seen peeling oranges with a mechanical peeler, then squeezing the juice! Tanner's was known for freshly squeezed orange juice and the ever-present accompaniment of red skin peanuts, nicely secured in a small wax paper bag and free with a drink. They also offered a delicious punch created by adding grape and pineapple juices to their squeezed orange juice. Their burgers were supreme. Any Charlotte native beyond a certain threshold age knows Tanners.

I photographed the S.H. Kress store in 1972, just before demolition began. Bank of America Plaza, now One South at The Plaza, was opened on the site in 1974. "Dime" stores or "five and dime" were the precursors of our modern Walmart/Dollar General stores. A shopper could have a full meal in most, buy basic tools, purchase a warm bag of various delicious nuts, find a package of twine or string, some basic clothing, shoes, jewelry, glue, and on and on it went. Kress offered a lunchroom with counters and seats on its lower level. It was famous for its "cornbread sticks" – cornbread cooked in a cast-iron cornbread tray, making the baked result look like an

Chapter 3 - Adventures Streetside: Downtown and Elsewhere

ear of corn. The stand-up counter on the street level was frequented by bus drivers, uptown workers, and bus traffic. Black people ordered at the very end of the counter near the donut maker, which offered a hot treat at almost any hour. Importantly for kids, they also carried a good selection of toys and model kits.

Frank Woolworth was considered the originator of the modern "dime" store. Dimes and nickels enabled him to build the tallest building, from 1913 until 1920, in the world in New York City. Woolworth was the class of the five and dimes. Woolworth occupied 112 -118 North Tryon. Its competitor, W.T. Grant, was located precisely where the Truist Tower courtyard meets North Tryon and next door to the present Foundation for The Carolinas, itself occupying the building of the former ladies' high fashion Montaldo's Store at 220 North Tryon. Montaldo's was an exclusive ladies' shop. Its front doors had vertical bars over their glass panels as if to say: "do not enter". Black Cadillacs – Sedan De Villes - were often parked in front of the store with chauffeurs standing watch. I was, of course, impressed by the vehicles – real class in my view.

Montaldo's later constructed an addition on its right side with a drive-through portal where limos could park off-street to let ladies exit without the inconvenience of weather. As a child, I had no opportunity or reason to enter Montaldo's. Finally, in 1978, I visited there to purchase a birthday dress and shoes for my wife Emily. Their attention to a gentleman shopping for a lady was remarkable, real class like the latter and original St. John of South Park.

Directly behind W. T. Grant was a Colonial Stores supermarket fronting 209 North College Street – about the present entrance to Truist Tower. As late as 1962, I shopped there and then rode the Number 13 bus home while holding two bags of groceries. Without a vehicle of my own, this was the way to go. All the drivers knew me and would stop in front of our duplex.

Liggett Rexall Drugs was on the northeast corner of the Square. Second to Kress, it was the busiest place near the Square. Like Kress, it had so many items needed by bus riders, and unlike Kress, it had a pharmacy–drug store in the lexicon of the time. Liggett had its "Rebel Room" offering both counter and seated dining, and was a favorite of bus drivers. At the opposite end of the block near Montaldo's was the City's premier theater – The

Carolina at 225. It was constructed in 1927 in the vaudeville era and before motion pictures with sound (talkies). It was the largest and most upscale of Charlotte's theaters, which we will cover in a later chapter.

Beyond Sixth Street, there was not a lot to attract my friends or me. I sometimes met friends, and we liked to ride the elevators at Belk's, Efird's, and Ivey's. Efird's was notable for both its older escalators and older elevators. The escalator treads were made of wooden slats! Their elevator outer doors were steel frames and wire glass, so shoppers waiting for an elevator or car/cab, as they are often called, could easily see both the cables and counterweights within their frames at the rear of the shafts. Belk's purchased Efird's in 1959/1960, and the older elevator equipment was on short notice.

Belk occupied almost the entire 100 block of North Tryon. Its original main building at 111-121 East Trade was noted for its "bargain basement", A smaller storefront called Belk annex, dedicated to shoes, was at 123 Trade. In 1958, a multistory addition, six stories and a basement with a sub-basement, was constructed at the corner of North College at 116–118 East Fifth Street. The land on the east side of College Street soon became a parking lot dedicated to Belk. Not so well known was the use of the sub-basement as a Civil Defense Fallout Shelter. I worked at Belk during my college years in the 1960s and had to visit the shelter space once. It was a literal warehouse of provisions. Its foundation wall along College Street was not removed with its demolition and is still in place, far below the surface.

Belk Bros. Co. was the corporate entity's name, but everyone in Charlotte knew it as Belk's. The store was a huge part of Charlotte's uptown commercial synergy, the cumulative total of which included J.B. Ivey, Martin's Department Store, multiple five-and-dime stores, and smaller department-type stores. Downtown Charlotte was, in fact, the consumer commercial center of a two-state region. The Sears relocation to 700 North Tryon only enhanced the variety with the addition of more square footage. Belk's was the biggest store, and when paired with Ivey's, it offered an impressive venue for shopping. The Fridays following Thanksgiving found the downtown area packed solid with shoppers and their vehicles. Cabs were busy and buses ran late.

Expansive suburban shopping malls were years away. Shopping in major

Chapter 3 - Adventures Streetside: Downtown and Elsewhere

cities was accomplished downtown. And Charlotte was large enough to have an iconic department store, and Belk's was it. Ivey's was not small, but Belk dominated its entire block following Efird's acquisition. At age five or six, I accompanied my grandmother—dressed in a suit, hat, and white gloves—on her downtown shopping trips. In the fifties, proper fashion for shopping was still the rule. We rode the No. 10 State Street bus. On the way downtown at the Turner Avenue intersection, we would cross the P&N tracks leading from Cedar Street yard to its primary freight yard at Pinoca, adjacent to Seaboard's yard. Yet another opportunity to see some railroad activity.

Once uptown and inside Belk's, patience was in order as my grandmother visited departments that were of little interest to me. She did a lot of sewing, and Belk's had part of its third floor dedicated to patterns, bolts of cloth, and all the accoutrements needed by a seamstress. She was not interested in the toy department until about October each year, so I had to spend time imagining I was playing with my friends among all the bolts of cloth. Belk also had a shoe repair shop, so sometimes we would make our way over to the smaller East Trade location.

FW Woolworth was next to Efird's (Belk's after 1959/60) on Tryon. There were two pass-throughs from Woolworth's to Belk's, one in the "basement" and one on the first floor. My grandmother's last stop before we went home was the nut and candy counter at Woolworth's. It was a 1950s edition of a chocolate shop with the addition of a variety of nuts, some of which rotated on a carousel under heat lamps. The heated cashews were a real treat. Woolworth was a premier dime store, a perfect combination of dollar store bargains, hardware, home goods, basic footwear, bath accessories, toys, jewelry, basic sporting goods, clothing, baby accessories, and hundreds of other things. On the first level, on the left side was a lunch counter for hungry shoppers. The downtown store closed when Belk's left downtown in 1988. I have a façade piece from the former W.T. Grant store and attempted to secure a storefront door pull plate debossed with Woolworths in red text, but came up short on that quest.

Belk offered multiple eating venues for its shoppers. The dining room on the top floor of Efird's was a full-service cafeteria. Another cafeteria was in the "basement" of the 1958 addition, where the workrooms for the

Blumenthal are located now. The mezzanine held the ladies' lounge adjacent to the lunch counter, which served burgers, sandwiches, etc. The lower-level (basement) cafeteria also offered two small private dining rooms available on a first-come, first-served basis. Friends and I used those private rooms into the 1980s.

Belk also had a somewhat remarkable communication system of pneumatic tubes that followed various routes throughout the store, connecting "service desks" with the central cash room. If small currency ($1s, $5s, $10s) were needed for a cash register, then larger paper currency was put into a small canister about the size of a frozen juice can and inserted into an outgoing pipe. In short order, change would be returned via an incoming pipe. Various types of refund paperwork and similar transactions were handled by the pneumatic system. Similar technology is in use today at drive-in banking centers.

Belk's had a large music department featuring both singles and albums. There was a portrait studio, a large toy department, and a comprehensive bookstore that lasted until almost the end. Boy Scout uniforms and accessories were on the fourth floor. Like most department stores, Belk's had a big layaway business. "Layaway" is a type of credit purchase where the purchaser pays for the goods before receiving them. It was in large measure a tool for holiday purchases, something like a Christmas savings club.

I especially enjoyed the ladies' fragrances department. After the 1958 addition, fragrances were located at the base of the mezzanine to maximize their traffic exposure. The sales ladies were always dressed impeccably. Mrs. Russell Campbell, wife of a bus driver, friend of my father, and Mrs. Mary Player worked there for years. Mrs. Player finally retired from Belk South Park in the 1970s.

For me and all my friends, Belk was part of our lives – it furnished our clothing, gave us a place to fill out our Saturdays after we departed movie theaters, a place to look forward to visiting – a part of growing up. The sprawling Belk's complex closed following the holiday season of 1988, 11 years after it had been connected to the "over street mall" pathway that winds through the center city business and retail district. A small namesake store for ladies resided for some years in the "over street mall" across the connecting corridor to the former Epic Center and just opposite Walgreens.

Chapter 3 - Adventures Streetside: Downtown and Elsewhere

Ivey's could not compare with Belk's in sheer size but was perceptively more upscale and did not count as heavily on its bargain basement attributes as its competitor. Ivey's offered its "Auto Park" garage, which was adjacent to the rear of the store on North Church Street. Drive in, exit the vehicle, shop, dine, and after shopping, wait while one's vehicle is retrieved. That was impressive indeed. The store offered only one dining venue, and it was quite upscale, the Tulip Terrace overlooking the Old Settlers' Cemetery. This was long before the arrival of Arthur's in the lower level. Founder Mr. JB Ivey lived at 1638 East Morehead. I remember it was an impressive, large home that was demolished following his passing. A medical building occupies the site today. Mr. Ivey had the storefront window's green shades lowered on Sundays. Belk did not. Storefront displays were an important element of advertising, and the larger stores had designated managers to regularly craft displays coordinated with their department's latest arrivals. Mrs. Eaton was responsible for Belk's storefronts.

My friends and I especially liked Ivey's because they had automatic elevators sooner than Belk. Until then, elevator operators ran each elevator. We liked to ride elevators after movies on Saturdays in an amateurish effort to meet girls. Of course, no one ever suggested what we might say if we had met girls.

My father bought shoes for me from a lady named Lucy Shoemaker, who worked in children's shoes in the basement. Like any large shoe store in the early 1950s, including Belk, there was a shoe fluoroscope available. Available from the 1930s until the 1950s, they offered a literal X-ray view of a child's feet inside his/her shoes. Promoted as a fitting device, it was more of a gimmick. Most were the size of a lectern. I would step up and put my feet in the two openings on the step. My father and the salesperson could look in viewing ports in the top side and see, in green relief, the bones of my feet inside the shoes. There were few, if any, standards for radiation or shielding from the various devices, and in our new atomic era, the fear of radiation overcame gimmickry, and the devices slowly disappeared.

Two other department stores of note were Ed Mellon Company at 106 West Trade (Marriott City Center resides there now) and Martins at 127 East Trade (entrance to Founders Hall/Bank of America Corporate Center). Martins was smaller than Belk and was gone by the early sixties. Ed Mellon

Company was a prestigious department store, smaller than Belk, and still in business when I graduated. There were others, but all relatively small – Stein's Men's Store, Bellas Hess, to name just two. In retrospect, it appears the massive enlargement of Belk's slowly but inexorably made Martins, Ed Mellon Co., and some others unprofitable. Ivey's building survived intact for repurposing, Belk and Martin's did not, and yielded their sites to Bank of America Corporate Center.

The 200 block of East Trade Street was an eclectic mix of secondary stores. Reliable Loan Company, Uncle Sam's Loan, Fligel's Men's Store, and Charlotte Army-Navy Store filled out the space now occupied by the Ritz Carlton. Reliable and its stablemates were sometimes called "pawn shop" row. In their small storefronts were displayed so many neat items that had been pawned for cash. I so badly wanted a pair of 7 x 50 binoculars to support my astronomy interests. Shortwave, and later, transistor radios about the size of a pack of cigarettes. I, of course, had little cash, so my quest was covetous, pure and simple.

The first two blocks of West Trade Street were busy venues for me. Richards Jewelers at 100 South Tryon also fronted Trade with its larger window, precisely where the city buses unloaded. In an era without the internet, department stores relied on newspaper ads and storefronts. And a big part of merchandising at the time was storefront display windows. Unlike department stores, jewelry store displays started at eye level, and they knew just how to capture a potential customer like me. I received a Kodak Brownie Hawkeye camera for Christmas one year. Its styling was purely form follows function, as if crafted by Raymond Lowey himself. At $12.95, including flash attachment, film, and flash bulbs, it was solid photo equipment. Richards' window displayed its companion Kodak "Bullseye". The Bullseye had an adjustable lens, and I liked accessories such as dials and knobs, but I lacked $18.95 – a lot of cash then! Richards was displaced by a park at the Square.

Steins Men's Store, Newberg's, and Rayless Dept Store were three of several storefronts west of Richards, which had been displaced by the early 1990s Interstate Tower. The Charlotte Theater later became Hooters. The New Yorker Restaurant at 125 and Miller's Central Hat Shop at 127 were two stops of choice for me. Both were displaced by a multi-tenant storefront that fills the space adjacent to the 129 West Trade Tower, formerly Wachovia Bank. It opened in December 57/January 58 and was the first new downtown tower since the Liberty Life Building in the 1920s before the Great Depression. There were five other towers outside the downtown area. Three of them are still extant. The Addison Building was constructed in 1926 on East Morehead at McDowell. Charlotte Memorial Hospital (Atrium) in 1939, Novant Medical Center (Presbyterian Hospital) in 1940, at Elizabeth and Hawthorne. In 1952 the Doctors Building on Kings Drive was demolished for new construction by Atrium. Law Building at 700 East Trade is now the site of the Law Enforcement Center

The Independence Trust Building anchored the Square at 100-102 West Trade. Built in 1909, its top two floors were added later. Like other "skyscrapers" of downtown, until central air conditioning could be retrofitted in the 1950s, window air conditioners dotted its classic façade. Its irregular floor plan facilitated circulation before central air conditioning became standard. The National Shirt Shop was its prime first-floor tenant.

I knew it was an old building, but its location was unbeatable. Physicians, insurance brokers, Woodmen of the World, Avon Cosmetics, dentists, including well-known Dr. Grady Ross, were on the tenant list. It was also a pit stop for me.

With a genesis perhaps dating to Charlotte's streetcar days, a large, convenient restroom/washroom was available for bus drivers in the substructure of the Independence Building. It was my pit stop when downtown. To reach it, I entered the lobby, walked past the elevators, turned down steps to a landing, and then another short flight of steps to the corridor by the boiler room, then a left turn at what must have been a small administrative area once used by Duke Power's uptown supervisors, then on to the washroom. When the building was constructed, this space extended beyond the sidewalk above to the edge of the curb adjacent to the street. Above were the vault lights, a nineteenth-century solution to illuminating subterranean spaces. Viewed from the sidewalk, it appeared as if hundreds of bottles of soft drinks were embedded in the concrete. This was nearly the case. Heat-strengthened glass, usually in circular shape and set in a metal frame, was level with the sidewalk and allowed natural light to reach the space below. The washroom, of course, had electric lights also.

The Independence Building was almost certainly the last survivor in the city center with sidewalk vault lights. The handsome building was demolished by implosion in October 1981. Repurposing was hardly in our commercial vocabulary at that time. Today, some of its façades would very likely have been incorporated into its replacement.

First Presbyterian Church, then as now, commanded the north side of West Trade's second block. On the opposite side was a representative collection of many businesses that served both bus traffic and the downtown population. The Grand Bohemian Hotel and the Carillon Building have deposed all those familiar storefronts of the 1950s and 1960s. The Piedmont Grill resided at 201 West Trade. It was pricier than the New Yorker. Next were New York Hatters and Cleaners, White Tower, Cay's Drugs, Kofinas Snack Bar, Carolina Cut Rate Drugs, Morris and Barnes Grocery, and the Hotel Charlotte, anchoring the corner with Poplar Street with a few smaller spaces in between.

Kofinas served beer, so I did not go there. However, the smell of draft beer and French fries that wafted out of its storefront doors was compelling to my olfactory senses. I often visited Morris and Barnes. Remarkably small for a grocery store, its clerks used a long pole grabber to reach the upper shelves, made necessary by its physical confines. It served both the uptown population and bus traffic. I shopped there often until I acquired my driver's license.

On the corner at 301 was Delmonico's Restaurant. My feet never touched inside its doors as its name alone was sufficient to deter those of lesser means. It went away with the demise of West Trade, and a tower now resides there. On the north side, near the marker denoting the former home of the late Mrs. Thomas "Stonewall" Jackson, was the Builders Building at 312-314. It dates to the mid-twenties and was an early site-cast concrete structure in the city. Throughout much of its early and midlife, it housed the offices of many building contractors, including the Associated General Contractors of America. A very small parcel at 316 between the Builders Building and Pine Street was the location of Sharon Oil Company, a service station, but also the terminal for Sharon Coach Company (see Chapter 6).

Across Pine Street and a couple of storefronts away was King's Business College. Union Bus Station at 416–424 (now a parking lot for The

Chapter 3 - Adventures Streetside: Downtown and Elsewhere

Kensington) was directly across the street from the Federal Court House and Post Office. There was a red sign with gold lettering above the entrance to the bus station with wording about loitering and solicitation. As to its meaning, my father's explanation was never clear to me.

The post office was only two blocks away from the Southern Railway Station (see Chapter 6) and was ideally located for a time when most mail was carried by rail. Geographically, these places were a bit beyond my normal range. The Langston-Moore dealership at 500 West Trade was of interest since I was and still am a car guy. 500 West Trade Apartments now occupies the site.

My father worked a "swing shift" for a couple of years and would get off work about 6:30. Sometimes I would go to a movie after school and then meet him for dinner at the New Yorker. To get home, we would board the No. 2 Green Street bus in front of First Presbyterian at the corner of Trade and Poplar. In the summer, there was usually a roar of cicadas in the big trees of the churchyard, and there was daylight until we finished dinner. Some evenings, we would see the New Orleans Express depart from the Union Bus Station. Greyhound assigned its best equipment to the Express – the GM PD-4501 Scenicruiser. It is the best-looking intercity bus ever made. Air-conditioned, partial double-decker with a restroom aboard, Greyhound ordered 1,000 of them. Some were still operational into the 1970s. Stainless steel siding and with twin GM Allison diesels. The bus would slowly enter Trade from the terminal exit alley and turn left as it did so, usually pulling widely to the left to make the immediate right turn onto South Mint Street. The slow, quick movements energized its GM air ride suspension, and the silver draft horse would slowly sway from side to side. When on Mint, the driver would stretch the throttle, and twin exhausts would exude authoritative black smoke with a sound that was irresistible to me. I thought it was class; it was and still is the best-looking bus in the world. That is why my friends and I loved the nation so much. We had the best, and it was a source of pride.

Beyond the Bobo Langston dealership building at 500 West Trade and North Graham was the Mecklenburg Hotel at 520-22. Across Trade was a collection of businesses serving rail travelers: several cafes, dry cleaners, a shoe repair, and a drug and sundries shop. The Southern Station was at

601 on the east side of the tracks. On the other side was a brick multi-story building housing Southern's local administrative office. I never walked there from the square, but the Presto Grill at 531 was of interest if only because of its name.

Tryon Street always seemed to have more importance than Trade, and to my young mind, South Tryon surpassed North Tryon for glitz. The tallest towers fronted South Tryon, and, until 1957, all the major banks. The Buster Brown Newsstand was my operating base. I knew both Al and Mr. Walker, who were the primary staffers. It was a long, narrow storefront. On one wall were magazines with newspapers from around the country filling a flat shelf the length of the magazine racks. In those days, news from other parts of the nation was best found in newspapers, which could be delivered to the newsstand within one day of their publication. The toilet at the rear was always available to me. Buster Brown was cool in the summer and warm in the winter. In winter, it was especially useful since the transit center of today was almost 40 years away, and bus riders awaited their routes on the street with no shelter from rain or barriers against the cold. I knew the bus schedules well, so I could minimize my time in the elements.

Between Buster Brown and the Liberty Life Building (later Baugh Building, now 112 South Tryon) were several addresses, including the National Hat Shop and Garibaldi and Bruns, the big name in jewelers. The Liberty Life Building was 20 stories and the tallest building in the state until Wachovia constructed a taller tower in Winston-Salem in 1960.

The First Citizens Bank Building now consumes all the linear footage once allocated to: Imperial Theater, Tate Brown Company, Bank of Charlotte, and Wachovia Bank. The Imperial closed in May 1964 when the Park Terrace Opened. The façade of the Wachovia Bank was salvaged when the building was demolished, and it was used as a cladding on a new structure at East Fourth and Caldwell Streets. Tate-Brown is only a memory for those young men who wanted to be cool. It was an "up-scale" men's store and the primary source of Gant button-down collar oxford shirts for those of us who attempted to emulate the extraordinarily attired Dick Van Dyke. For me, it is still questionable just what advantages Gant shirts offered, and at $5.99 each, it was a financial stretch. Belk's Archdale label at $3.99 each was my brand of choice.

Chapter 3 - Adventures Streetside: Downtown and Elsewhere

The opposite side of the first block of South Tryon started with S.S. Kress and ended with Union National Bank at 139. In between were the Tryon Theater, Rex Billiards (I wasn't allowed there and subsequently only learned pool later in life), Tanners at 123, and Simpsons Photos at 129. If I could afford a roll of 620 film for my Brownie Hawkeye and once its twelve exposures had been committed to the many useless objects on my photo list, I would drop it off at Simpsons for processing into black and white prints. Several days later, I would be able to see just how wasted my photos were. If only I had that Kodak Bullseye with the adjustable lens.........

In 1960, construction on a new building – the Cutter Building - was begun on that southeast corner of Tryon and Fourth Street. Only building permit records could identify whether it, or the new North Carolina National Bank tower at 200 South Tryon, was the first new tower with contemporary glass and curtain wall cladding. The Cutter Building was the pride of real estate developer John King Cutter. Some days, friends and I would go downtown after classes ended at "old" Harding High School and watch the construction activities. It was a time when litigation was a lesser threat, and businesses wanted the public to see what they were building. In fact, general contractors often built wooden sidewalk covers with artwork on the sidewalls with openings for passers-by to view the site activities. Directly across from the Cutter Building, the new North Carolina National Bank tower was beginning. Each had a lower pedestal base from which a tower arose. NCNC was the taller of the two, and its lower façade was of beautiful granite. That was in the fall of 1960, and twenty years afterwards, I would be working in the former Cutter Building, known then as the BarclaysAmerican Building.

The Cutter Building story illustrates how an office building experiences regeneration. The fifth floor of the Cutter opened onto the roof of the lower floors, which could be used by its primary tenant – American Credit - which in 1979 became BarclaysAmericanCorporation (yes, one word). The Charlotte Athletic Club had formerly occupied its lower level. When Barclays Bank purchased it, the "basement" was repurposed into the "Promenade," and a monumental stair, visible from the 4th Street sidewalk, led directly to the new boardroom.

I had the pleasure of working there beginning in 1980, and it was the cleanest building in the city under Barclays' occupancy. At the time, parking in the generous 10-foot-wide parking spaces of Southern National Center was a mere $35 monthly with my discount of five dollars. A pedestrian connector over the alley running between 3rd and 4th Streets provided access to the rear of the Barclays Building. Those who occupied the upper floors had no reason to worry about prompt elevator service. Leroy, in a buttoned jacket and tie, was in the lobby to hold doors open to ensure each of the elevators was filled to its capacity. The experience was first class. Some twenty years later, soon after Barclays' departure, the entire building was stripped down to its concrete structure and completely modernized – a third iteration. I believe it is the only tower that has a cantilevered floor without exterior columns to interrupt office space.

Kale Lawing office outfitters at 227-229 was a fixture on that block, as was the Broadway/Fox theater and Thacker's Cafeteria. At the Third Street corner was the Wilder Building, now the site of a Marriott Courtyard. The Wilder Building was well known as on its 4th floor was the studio of WBT, then a premier radio station and one of the "50,000-watt clear channel stations" allowed by the FCC. The main Western Union office was in a storefront on its ground floor. It was a time when one might occasionally witness a telegram being delivered. It was also a means to send money quickly by wire. Telegrams were an alternative to long-distance calls.

The Johnston Building at 212 was constructed in 1924, and both it and the Liberty Life Building were modernized in the 1980s. They were the city's two tallest for decades and represented the classic pre-WWII style urban towers. The 300 South Tryon Barings Tower now occupies the former site of Jack Wood Ltd., men's clothiers. The Jefferson Standard Life Building was and still is across the street at 301. The Union National Bank was on its first floor. Renovated several times, it was designed by J.N. Pease Associates and is now a part of Wells Fargo. Latta Arcade, a National Historic Site, still resides at 322, and behind it is Brevard Court. The YMCA held the corner at 330 South Tryon until it relocated to East Morehead near the end of the 1950s decade. Stutts News Service and Myers Service Station – perhaps the closest gas station to the Square - were located at 410–414, sites now occupied by the 400 South Tryon tower and the Bechtler Museum of Fine Art.

Chapter 3 - Adventures Streetside: Downtown and Elsewhere

My movement this far south was usually to see new cars. Then as now, St. Peter's Catholic Church began the 500 block on Tryon's east side at 501. A few yards away at 522 was Frank Woods Pontiac. Yes, a new car showroom only four blocks from the Square. Its showroom could hold two or three vehicles at most. The site is now occupied by the 550 South Tryon tower. It was at Frank Woods that I saw my first Pontiac Grand Prix – a 1962 Catalina body with minimalist trim but with nice bucket seats, a console with floor shift, and a 389. Cu In V-8 equipped with a four-barrel carburetor and dual exhausts. For some unknown purpose, rather than a tachometer on the console, it carried a manifold vacuum gauge. As my friend Jack Washam said of the Grand Prix: "How to win friends and influence people".

City Chevrolet was located at 710 South Tryon. And yes, there was another dealer – Folger Buick at 900. These, and other uptown dealers – among them Heath Ford, later to become Young Ford on West Fifth Street. Pettit Ford, on East Fourth, where the Federal Reserve Building is now, later became Town and Country Ford. Pyramid Chevrolet (later Don Allen) on the corner of East Trade and Davison, like the others, exited the center city. As it turned out, Young Ford relocated to the corner of East Stonewall and South Brevard Street in 1960, where the Convention Center is today. That was at the south end of the former Southern Railway freight terminal area. Purportedly, there was in the early twentieth century a coal gasification plant on that site. Young's used car lot was across Brevard, now the site of the NASCAR Hall of Fame. Brevard was the western perimeter of Second Ward, often known as Brooklyn, which urban renewal removed/destroyed in the 1960s. A couple of homes were just north of the lot, facing Brevard into the early 1960s.

A word about automobiles. In the 50s and in the 60s, auto manufacturers restyled their vehicles every two or three years. To keep up with the latest styling, those who had the financial resources, and a lot who did not, purchased new vehicles on the same two- or three-year cycle. We all loved those cars, and they are dear to auto junkies today. Automobile showrooms were exciting places. In truth, vehicles of the 1950s and early 1960s needed more care and more frequent maintenance than contemporary autos. Automobile brakes were relatively poor, tire technology was marginal, fuel mileage was terrible, most gasoline had lead additives, and safety features were almost non-existent. Tires of those days were not capable of providing the solid handling that we take for granted today. It was not uncommon to see a driver stopped on the shoulder of a road descending a steep mountain grade to let the vehicle's brakes cool. Nevertheless, Americans were taken by their vehicles and dutifully followed Detroit marketing.

Some car enthusiasts posit that the 1949 Oldsmobile 88 with its new overhead valve V-8 engine was the first modern "street muscle car". Possibly, however, it benchmarked a horsepower race that continued for over two decades. Short street acceleration contests were not uncommon and, on some streets, almost guaranteed. They were not quarter drag mile races but rather brief sprints to see who could prevail. It was about bragging rights. New vehicles appeared in dealer showrooms during September, and potential buyers would visit to inspect their latest gadgetry and engine options. Detroit threw out names like Turbo-Thrust, Swept Wing Design, Turbo-Hydramatic, Cruise-O-Matic, Wide Track, Super Turbine 400, or Advanced Thrust, which were only marketing monikers but terms to which consumers predictably responded.

Chapter Notes

Downtown and Uptown: 1950 Charlotte Telephone Directory: Four listings for "downtown", no "uptown" listings. 1964 Charlotte Telephone Directory; 4 listings of "downtown", 2 listings of "downtowner"; no "uptown" listings. Between 1950 and 1963 it was known as downtown. The shift to uptown began in the 1970s/80s and was gradual but unstoppable although one will still hear downtown from time to time.

Shoe Fluoroscopes: From the 1930s until the 1950s X-Ray shoe fitting machines were popular in department stores and shoe stores. They looked like a lectern with a couple of steps, the top riser of which had two openings for one's feet. The top of the cabinet had three viewing ports for a salesperson (and parents since they were largely used in fitting children's shoes), and the buyer. The idea was to use X-Rays to show bones within the shoes being worn to help determine the proper fit. The American Standards Association set exposure levels in 1946. Going forward, especially in the Atomic age when radiation exposure became a big concern, the use and popularity of the machines began to decline. They were gone by the end of the 1950s.

BarclaysAmericanCorporation: Barclays Bank of England acquired American Credit Corporation, a Charlotte company wholly owned by Wachovia Bank, in 1979. Consumer credit, factoring, and mortgage services were part of its portfolio. BAC fully renovated the ACC Building, formerly the Cutter Building, at 201 South Tryon. The project was completed in 1980. I had the honor of working for Gary Williams in its Real Estate Department. My colleague was a man of supreme diplomacy, Julian Johnson. It was a class corporation with the cleanest building in Charlotte. When a gentleman left his floor, it was understood that his suit coat would be on. At the time ladies wore dresses, no slacks, believe it or not. It was an unforgettable and fondly rememberable experience.

For three decades **S. H. Kress** was the iconic corner anchor of Independence Square. The photo was shot in 1972 a short while before the store closed and the site was razed for the new 40 story NCNB tower and adjacent the Raddison Hotel tower. Photo: Author's Collection.

Contemporary photo of the former S. H. Kress location. The tower is now known as One South at The Plaza, the adjacent hotel is now The Omni. Drivers continue to ignore the turn prohibition signs in all approaches. In the 1950s and 1960s when a police officer was assigned to the square he would step out and with a loud blast of his whistle correct the errant motorist. CMPD Office Charlie Walker carried on that tradition until he retired in the early 2000s. - Google photo.

The **100 Block of North Tryon** as it looked just beyond the Independence Building. It is likely the Christmas season of 1955. The large Christmas Seals cross is visible as are light decorations. The most recent discernable automobile is a 1956 Chevrolet Bel Aire that appears directly under the Christmas Seals' cross and slightly ahead of the No. 5 Dilworth bus. Baker's Shoes was located at 109 North Tryon only a few yards south of McLellan's Five and Dime. The two buses are former Duke Power GMC "old looks" finishing their first year of service under the management of City Coach Lines. No 5 Dilworth is a peak hour only route. The second bus is No. 16 York Road. Photo: Robinson Spangler Carolina Room, Public Library of Charlotte-Mecklenburg County.

Contemporary view of the **100 Block of North Tryon**. The Independence Building was dropped by demolition explosives in October 1981. One Independence Center and the adjacent Marriott City Center soon replaced the structures that fronted both North Tryon and West Trade Streets. Food vendors, and sidewalk dining, were seldom, if ever, present in the 1950s. Food and flower vendors have been contemporary center city fixtures for several decades. Google Photo

The Square at an early 1960s Christmas Parade (Carolinas Carrousel Parade). At the time parades began at East/West/South Blvd intersection, north on South Blvd., and then left onto East Morehead and then right onto South Tryon, ending at the Sears parking lot at 700 North Tryon. Trailways buses are being used to block the West Trade side of the Square. The band is from Harry P. Harding High School. The Liberty Life Building at 112 is barely visible on the extreme left of the photo. Between Buster Brown Newsstand and 112 were Brownlee Jewelers owned by future Mayor Al Russo, Hanover Shoes, and jeweler Garibaldi and Bruns that lasted long enough to be an original tenant in South Park. Photo: Author's collection.

The Square from about the same angle. All the storefronts from Richard's Jewelers to the 112 South Tryon Building (former Liberty Life, Baugh Building with its archway) have been gone for decades. A park exists there now. Google photo.

The **Square** looking toward North Tryon. It is clearly summertime. The two ladies are about to cross in front of a 1958 Plymouth. Efird's logo is emblazoned on the south side of its massive department store building indicating it has not yet been absorbed by competitor Belk. The photo is either 1958 or 1959. F. W. Woolworth five and dime is immediately adjacent to Efird's. In the distance the brick almost windowless building with a wide light colored horizontal sign is the exclusive Montaldo's women's store. The taller building in the far distance is the Hotel Wm. R. Barringer. The large WBTV signage atop Liggett's Rexall Drugs provided continuous time and temperature. An unusual scene as there are no city buses in sight. Photo: Robinson Spangler Carolina Room, Public Library of Charlotte- Mecklenburg County.

The author at age 11 inside the **Buster Brown Newsstand** at 102 South Tryon, immediately next door to Richard's Jewelers. Had I received the Brownie Bullseye camera I really wanted this photo would have been of higher quality. The entire lower shelf of the display was lined with newspapers. In the 1950s printed media was the primary source of information and there was many news dealers scattered uptown. Turns out I was wearing the warmest coat I had in that decade. Photo: Author's collection.

Northwest view. Taken from atop Jefferson First Union Tower (now Wells Fargo) in summer 1972 virtually replicates the view as it would have looked in 1963 excepting the ACC signage. Photo: Author's collection.

Legend
A – 129 West Trade – Wachovia
B – 200 South Tryon – NCNB
C – 112 South Tryon
D – 201 South Tryon – American Credit Company
E – 100 West Trade – Imploded October 1981.

Northwest view. Contemporary photo taken from slightly higher elevation and using the same symbology. Four of the five towers shown in the previous photo survive, including the pre-depression classic 112 South Tryon Building (D). Google Earth photo.

Miller's Central Hat Shop. There is no better example of a direct and visible connection with the streetside than Miller's Central Hat Shop. The shop was located at 127 West Trade, next to the New Yorker Restaurant at 125 and only two doors from the Charlotte Theater at 123. I remember the shoeshine guy on the right, so this photo was probably taken between 1955 and 1960. The shine rack was tall even for an eleven or twelve-year-old kid like me. There were usually 2 or 3 shine guys on duty. Two of them, Pop and Richard, I remember well. It was a busy place.

A little farther back on the right were the dressing booths where one could await having slacks or a suit pressed. Most men wore hats then and a large segment of Miller's business was cleaning and blocking hats in addition to dry cleaning. John G. Miller is on the left, leaning over the counter and his son is standing a short distance back. Miller was an original member of the Charlotte Chamber of Commerce and its longest running member when he passed away in 1982. The shine rack is still in the family. Photo: Courtesy Miller Family/Jim Turner.

Then and now. Knight Publishing Building (Charlotte Observer/Charlotte News) completed 1969. The building replaced a previous building but survived less than fifty years on this site just south of the earlier Observer Building. A Southern Railway track once crossed at this location to reach the Southern Depot. The second photo is the view with a new tower construction underway. Aurthor's collection/Google photo.

All Aboard for Gastonia. A difference of 80 years. The Piedmont & Northern passenger depot was only four blocks from The Square. For decades it served as an interurban rail connection with Gaston County. South Mint Street is just on the other side of the shrubs on the far right. The Depot itself is on a corner just beyond bounded by Mint and West Fourth Streets. The present Charles R. Jonas Federal Court House (once the site of a US Mint) in the background. The main US Post Office was then housed in the Court House building. Photo: Used with Permission of Golden West Books, Piedmont and Northern, The Great Electric System of the South, 1974.

Truist Field resides where P&N once had a freight yard. The white outlined area is the location of the P&N Depot of the previous photo. Google photo.

Another 80 years of changes. About 1940. P&N Railway used an overhead electric catenary just like present day streetcars. One of their electric locomotives is in the left foreground. The Mint Street freight depot is directly ahead with two box cars at its docks. The building in the distance is the Hotel Charlotte. The Liberty Life (112 South Tryon) Building is the tall structure in the right background. The depot is at the corner of Third and Mint Streets. Directly across Mint Street is the Juvenile Detention Quarters. Homes from the turn of the century are still extant around the center city and three houses are visible on Mint. Photo: Used with Permission of Golden West Books, *Piedmont and Northern, The Great Electric System of the South*, 1974.

1957 Desirables. Considered by some car buffs the most desired 1957 automobile in the United States was the Chevrolet Bel-Aire convertible. And there are a lot of arguments about that. This contemporary example appears partially restored, it has neat rubber tipped bumper guards, full wheel covers with spinners, and rocker panel chrome trim. It no doubt has the "Turbo-Fire" 283 Cu. In. small block V-8 with a four-barrel carburetor, and dual exhausts. In keeping with the advertising of the times, there was absolutely nothing about the vehicle that involved a 'Turbo'. Photo: Author's Collection

1957 Dodge Custom Royal. Immaculate gray and silver with the Royal Lancer wheel covers. This example appeared to be perfect. The D-500 option offered 325 or 354 Cu. In. hemi engines from 285 to 340 horsepower. Not many were ordered. Very few automobiles could match a D-500's acceleration. When Broderick Crawford of the TV show Highway Patrol put his foot in it, one could see what a Dodge could do. Dodge had the most attractive fins of any Chrysler car. Photo: Author's collection.

Changing skyline. This 2016 photo depicts three of the landmarks (two former locations and one present building) of the previous photo. Romere Bearden Park is across Mint Street beyond the bleachers. Photo: Aurthor's collection.

Belk, 1958 Addition. Except for some updated appointments and shopper's fashions, this is how the Belk 4th floor looked for its entire existence. Lay aways, phonograph records, toys, and some house wares were on this floor. The down escalator is at the very left corner of the photo. There was a time when many women made clothing. Patterns, cloth bolts, and sewing accessories were at this same location on the 3rd floor. Many years later from this same point on the 2nd floor shoppers, and the uptown population, could connect with the Overstreet Mall when it opened in 1977. Photo: Author's collection.

For those who remember Belk. This is a view taken from Belk's mezzanine lunch counter in 1988 not long before the center city store closed to make way for BOA Corporate Center. A 100-year anniversary banner for Belk mounted to the column on the right side. The escalators are barely discernable in the left rear background. For years this area had the best uptown bookstore. Photo: Author's collection.

Belk had it all. Through much of the downtown's existence through the 1980s, one could purchase about anything there. Combined with adjacent F. W. Woolworth and Liggett's Rexall Drugs on the Square it was a super service center. Even in this 1988 photo a large selection of furniture was available on the 4th floor and this young lady took advantage of it. Photo: Author's collection.

Chapter 4
Charlotte's Premiere Street – Independence Boulevard

Background

Independence Boulevard is the road that had to be built and the one that should never have been built. When it worked well one could rocket from Wilkinson Blvd to the coliseum area almost without stopping. It delivered fans to the gates of Memorial Stadium. It moved tanker trucks from the Paw Creek tank farm to eastern Carolina destinations. Anyone who drove a vehicle in our city in the fifties, sixties, seventies, eighties or nineties almost certainly knew Independence. It was praised and cursed. There were protests in the 1940s against it. It split three well defined neighborhoods, generated exhaust from lead gasoline that wafted into front doors, destroyed a public rose garden, and had engineering features that some might consider bordering on criminal today. Originally it had no turn lanes. On its eastern end it became so commercialized it generated its own culture. It was handy. It was needed. It took years to replace and undo its damage.

In the 1960s I often worked for my uncle at his Gulf Station at I-85/ Little Rock Road. Travelers would, for instance, often ask how to reach Presbyterian Hospital, or some other destination. Invariably we directed them down Little Rock to Wilkinson, then left at Wilkinson Boulevard, continue onto Independence, and at the thirteenth traffic signal, turn right. Presbyterian would be dead ahead. Independence was the way to go, just count traffic signals and turn accordingly.

We all knew Charlotte was the strategic hub of the Carolinas, Charlotte was a centroid in the north-south (US29, US 21) and east-west (US 74) primary highway network. By the 1940s, it was clear that a more efficient US 74 was needed. It was the mountains to coast route through the state. To traverse Charlotte from the east drivers entered the city on Monroe Road/ East Seventh Street, then used McDowell, Church, or Graham Streets to connect with Morehead Street that carried them westward to Wilkinson Boulevard

From the west it was in reverse order. For context, US 29, a Washington – Atlanta route, skirted downtown via Graham Street to Morehead. Its ultimate successor would become I-85, and the Federal-Aid Highway Act of 1944 was its genesis. Independence also sprang from the same Federal funding initiative.

The first or eastern phase was opened in 1949. It was this phase that did the most damage to the landscape. The second phase was completed by 1956/57. It was through less developed land on the westside but was still impactful, especially to a small pocket of residences around Pope Street. Remarkably two residential structures from the area survive on Dunbar Street. The name Independence now exists only to define the US 74 East Expressway. On the west end the Wilkinson name now extends to I-77 where it loses its identity. The original elevated section that passed by Charlotte Pipe and Foundry becomes West Carson Blvd that continues to South Boulevard Its previous right of way follows South Blvd to South Caldwell Street where the original alignment began a tangent from the big curve to the former Thompson Orphanage pasture (later Charlottetown Mall and now occupied by The Metropolitan/Target). It is now called East Brooklyn Village Avenue. Then the original concrete roadway – literally the original concrete pavement - becomes Charlottetown Avenue until it reaches Seventh Street where it transitions to the Independence Expressway, the namesake's only remaining legacy.

Birth of The Idea

Following his three terms as mayor, Mr. Ben Douglas Sr. became a leading protagonist for building Independence Boulevard which was eligible for Federal funding under the Federal- Aid Highway Act of 1944. The city's leading design firm, J.N. Pease Associates, was commissioned by city manager James Marshall to assist with the routing of a new crosstown road. In its internal History of Pease document, engineer Russ Westmoreland described working with Marshall and how they crafted a route through the miles long maze of streets. The Federal design criteria as noted in Westmoreland's narrative are indeed noteworthy:

Chapter 4 - Charlotte's Premiere Street – Independence Boulevard

1. The new road must provide access from one side of the city to the other.
2. It must approach but not enter the downtown area.
3. It must aid in slum clearance.
4. It must provide access to public recreation areas.
5. The municipality must adopt a long-range improvement plan.

Independence Boulevard met each of the pre-requisites. Subsequent decades have shown the far-ranging consequences Item 3 had for both Charlotte and many cities. So many times, I heard someone refer to Brooklyn as a slum. I certainly did not understand urban planning in the fifties, but I did know "that slum" was home to a lot of people. I knew Brooklyn better than those who had never been there. It was the eastern end of my father's No 7-bus route. I remember him maneuvering the 102-inch-wide No. 1002 through its crowed streets. Brooklyn was a Black neighborhood and somewhat a city within a city.

It did not look like my neighborhood and there was at least one street that was neither paved nor had curb and gutter. It was a contiguous neighborhood with churches, two schools, and businesses to support its residents. While a coherent neighborhood, there were deficiencies that were not positive and by a reasonable standard needed attention. Independence will likely always be remembered for its impact on neighborhoods of color. However, it was an equal opportunity disrupter. Those who lived in Elizabeth or Chantilly would certainly have agreed. Geographically Brooklyn was in the way of the center city's growth and Independence was likely viewed only as the first step of the "slum clearance" as part of a longer-term redevelopment strategy. The moniker of "urban renewal" was used to create a positive image. Given the wholesale disruption of a community, a fundamental question might be in order: what promises were made and which were kept.

The construction of Independence coincided with the first three decades that Herman J. Hoose served as Charlotte's Director of Traffic Engineering from 1948 until 1978. Hoose was a nationally recognized innovator under whose leadership the existing older street network became more efficient. One-way streets and reversible lanes were part of the improvements attributable to him. Charlotte streets are mostly random and not gridded, which complicated his challenges.

Geography

Let us begin in 1957 at the intersection of West Morehead Street and Wilkinson Boulevard. Dowd Road was the earlier direct artery from downtown westward to Gastonia. Later, West Morehead supplanted Dowd and became the primary route. Phase 2 intersected Morehead-Wilkinson immediately adjacent to the Gondola Restaurant (now a cigar bar). Driving eastward, Independence ran downhill into the Stewart/Irwin creek basin where it connected with Walnut Avenue (now an extension of Freedom Drive) and then with Summit Avenue. From there it climbed over South Clarkson and past the Charlotte Pipe Foundry very much as it (now Wilkinson) does today. Then over the Southern Railway tracks, taking out Pope Street (a small Black neighborhood), it dropped to a grade intersection with South Mint Street. There was a short straightaway before it curved to meet South Church. This is part is still in place. It reversed its curve and climbed to intersect South Tryon Street. So far it created minimal damage to the built environment, except for a small residential pocket surrounding Pope Street.

Crossing Tryon there was an off ramp to South Boulevard The roadway rose over the south lanes of South Boulevard and made a ninety-degree left turn over what once had been the northbound lanes of South Boulevard before it dropped quickly under East Morehead. The ramp from South Boulevard was so short to be laughable today. In retrospect, it is difficult to believe the combination curve and elevation change packed into that small footprint. The road then dropped into the bottom land and rose again to intersect Stonewall Street where it made about a sixty-degree right bend and then, on the tangent path of former East Stonewall Street, ran straight through the Brooklyn neighborhood. Tractor trailer trucks always used the center lane and local drivers learned when near a truck to lay back as the trailers could not remain in their lane when making the curve eastbound.

Brooklyn was a contiguous, self-sufficient Black neighborhood, the history of which has been thoroughly documented. There was a row of "shotgun" houses on the south side of the new roadway just feet from six lanes of concrete and they remained for many years. The pride of the community, Second Ward High School was on the north side of Independence and a tunnel was constructed underneath so students could safely cross the street.

Chapter 4 - Charlotte's Premiere Street – Independence Boulevard

The entrances are gone; the tunnel may still be entombed under the existing roadway.

Once my father took my grandfather and me to South McDowell to see the road construction. There was a building near the right-of-way of the new road and it had been raised with special jacks, and very large logs were in place under the building. The building was subsequently rolled to the south side where it remained for several decades. An apartment building is standing there today. Brooklyn had fifteen years of life remaining before urban renewal and during that time it coexisted with Independence.

Independence continued through the Brooklyn streets on the east side of McDowell then went into another creek bottom as it split the pasture of Thompson Orphanage. My dad would show me their dairy cows as we passed there. The chapel of the orphanage is now a venue between Third and Fourth Streets. Independence then skirted the Cherry neighborhood (also Black), taking out Cecil Street and the north end of Cherry Street. Some houses were left occupied and remarkably close to the roadway. It then intersected East Fourth Street before reaching Elizabeth Avenue (the present Third Street connector was not in place then). Fox Street was taken out and became a memory as the boulevard continued east. Memorial Stadium was just ahead and on fall Friday evenings or Shrine Bowl Saturdays, Independence fulfilled one design purpose by delivering thousands to the biggest stadium around.

Just beyond Seventh Street, Independence obliterated the Sunnyside Rose Garden which purportedly had thousands of rose bushes. It then continued eastward splitting off the northern side of the Elizabeth neighborhood. The roadway crested at Hawthorne Lane, and in a sweeping "S" curve dropped and then via a high bridge rose over the Seaboard RR tracks, quickly and dangerously bringing speeding traffic downgrade to a traffic signal at Pecan Avenue. The Hawthorne intersection held a landmark for decades – the Krispy Kreme coffee shop on its southeast corner. From Pecan the six lanes of concrete replaced two lanes of the former Westmoreland Avenue. Our Lady of Consumption Catholic Church on Shenandoah Avenue had guard rails around its playground which was only a few feet away for Independence. Homes on either side became elevated above the road which was at a lower grade elevation. Many had concrete retaining walls securing their original front lawns, necessitating that homeowners drive out rather than back out of their driveways into the busy roadway.

Another sweeping "S" curve at Morningside Drive and the Independence right-of-way moved from the former Westmoreland Avenue to the Chesterfield Avenue. In a long straightaway it ran past Briar Creek Road and Briar Creek Baptist Church on its north side corner, passed the Charlotte Coliseum, David Ovens Auditorium, and what would soon become a long commercial strip that was something of a linear community and often a rush hour traffic nightmare. The roadway had to climb upgrade, curve slightly to the right, and it was then a straight shot to Monroe once the new four lane route from Monroe was completed. Until then, Old Monroe Road (Charlotte Highway) connected to Independence beyond Idlewild Road on an alignment that later became Conference Drive. Charlotte native Russ Rodgers worked on a team that mowed the shoulders and median for the first time in 1955.

One Route to Everywhere

I drove Independence regularly – in fact from 1967 until 1980 every weekday. From 1962 until its rebuilding into a freeway in the 1990s my wheels knew its concrete surface. I know of no other roadway that became so much a part of so many commuter pathways. No other east-west route traversed the city with its efficiency or intersected the many streets that sprang from its trunk like so many limbs. I often picked up my father at the City Coach garage at East Eleventh and North Brevard Streets. To go home it was south on Brevard to just past Young Ford at Brevard and Stonewall (now East Brooklyn Village Avenue) where an extremely short on ramp let us engage Independence just before it went under East Morehead. Then we did the ninety-degree right curve that put us on a west heading. Past Tryon, past Charlotte Pipe and Foundry, through the Summit Avenue intersection, on to Walnut Avenue (now an extension of Freedom Drive). We stopped at Wilkinson/Morehead where we usually grabbed a copy of the *Charlotte News* from one of the young paper guys waving at the stopped vehicles. We were home in three more minutes.

The Fifth Street connector was created so center city traffic could slingshot onto the original Independence Boulevard which is now

Chapter 4 - Charlotte's Premiere Street – Independence Boulevard

Independence Freeway. In 1972 Brookshire Freeway (named for Mayor Stanford Brookshire) provided the I-85/Westside connection to east US 74 so at last the Paw Creek tankers had a faster, more direct, and presumably safer route through the city.

When working at J. N. Pease Associates (2925 East Independence) it was often necessary to visit Code Enforcement or a client such as Duke Power. Independence was a fast ride to my destination. When Independence's stars aligned, it was possible to reach the airport parking lot in thirty-five minutes. When it worked, it worked well.

The Culture of Independence

My first direct engagement with Independence was in 1961. My uncle Bob Winchester and his friend Ralph Schrum went into the service station business in 1960 and purchased the Esso (later Exxon) station at Plaza and Eastway Drive. The next year my uncle became a sole owner/dealer when he acquired the Esso station at Elizabeth Avenue and Independence (somewhat later Schrum owned the Cotswold Gulf station for decades and was one of the best-known dealers in the city). There were two Esso stations at the Elizabeth intersection. The other was on the southwest corner (where CPCC Levine Technology Building is today) and only two hundred feet from the house of author Harry Golden. A CPCC parking garage is there now. Bob Winchester soon acquired that station also, "cornering" the market at that location.

The first location was a small, two-bay building on a shallow and narrow lot where CPCC Levine Health Sciences Building resides now. He had a solid customer base of both businesses and residents of Elizabeth and Myers Park. A few yards away on Elizabeth Avenue was Douglas Furs, one of the businesses begun by former Mayor Ben Douglas, Sr. whose Douglas and Sing Mortuary was on the corner of Fox Street and Elizabeth Avenue – squarely in the path of the new roadway. That circumstance and Douglas's strong advocacy for Independence fed some interesting side bar conversations.

In the summer of 1961, I worked Saturdays for Bob washing cars. Douglas had a new 1961 Lincoln Continental. It was an elegantly clean and understated design by Elwood Engel with minimalist chrome and none of the flashy fins and accoutrements of its contemporaries. It set the mark on its way to three decades of quality design and styling until its market changed in the 1990s. It was my great pleasure to take it out of our washing bay and detail it. The design was and still is exquisite.

I had ample time to observe Independence. There were many homes around the area including East Fifth Street, which ran through what is now the quadrangle of CPCC's central campus. Houses were on each side of the street. The massive oak tree in the quadrangle once grew in someone's East Fifth Street backyard. Homes still existed on Elizabeth which is the spine of the college campus. In retrospect it seems there was little concern of how adjacent commercial development might affect pre-war neighborhoods. At the time traffic was heavy on the boulevard, or so I thought. There were no turn lanes, which by today's standards would be unthinkable.

The neighborhood east and uphill of Central High School, now CPCC's Central Building, ran all the way to Hawthorne. In 1961 it was still filled with homes. Park Drive ran up the steep hill adjacent to Memorial Stadium and its houses fronted the stadium just across the street. Its residents certainly saw a lot of action. By 1968 CPCC buildings occupied or were under construction on the blocks between Park Drive and Elizabeth and between Kings Drive (now Pease Lane and formerly Cecil Street). The sole remaining residential structure today is at the corner of Torrence Street and Elizabeth. It is occupied by a law firm. Remarkably Fox Street survives in the form of a short length that runs by the Auto Bell Car Wash at East Third and Charlottetown Avenue, terminating at a short, isolated stretch of East First Street in the Cherry neighborhood. Pride & Joy Day Care occupies much of its curb frontage. If projected eastward this short stub of Fox Street aligns with the former Independence Boulevard which followed the original Fox Street right-of-way. One original house remains at the corner of Fox and Charlottetown Avenue.

Jerry's Drive-In Restaurant was at the corner of Fourth and Independence. It later became The Athens Restaurant which served customers 24 hours a day. Late nights would see it full of patrons and hungry police officers. The CPCC Shaw Building stands on the site today. The real commercial culture of Independence was the high-density strip between Briar Creek Road and North Sharon Amity Road. We knew nothing of neighborhood service centers, or mixed-use commercial centers in those days. Except for

Chapter 4 - Charlotte's Premiere Street – Independence Boulevard

Charlottetown Mall, Park Road Shopping Center, Central Square, Freedom Village, or Cotswold Shopping Center consumers shopped downtown or in smaller strip centers.

For a road that was designed to facilitate traffic flow Independence seemed to go the other direction. Independence put all the retail businesses one might want or need into one long commercial strip that began with what is now Paul Buck Boulevard and continued to Pierson Drive. There were no service roads, and those visiting restaurants, stores, and shops used Independence for access. Traffic signals at Westchester, Woodland, and Pierson intersections funneled traffic from residential areas north of Independence directly into Coliseum Shopping Center (Westchester) and into Amity Gardens Shopping Center (Woodland, Pierson). The Coliseum Center was a linear strip facing Independence. It had among other retail shops, a K-Mart, a Park 'N Shop, a 24-hour Eckerd Drugs (with a lunch counter), and the only Army-Navy store in east Charlotte. Amity Gardens offered the Louis and Son department store, in its early days a Woolworth, a Revco drug store, and a Barclays cafeteria. Clarks (later Cooks/later Haverty's), a competitor of K-Mart, occupied an out-parcel site in the general area of present-day Walmart. Farther out beyond Sharon Amity there were multiple auto dealers. For instance, Folger Buick and City Chevrolet had relocated from downtown. In 1964 the Capri Theatre opened just west of K-Mart thereby putting a first-class movie house much closer to the area.

Considered as a whole, the retail culture of Independence was comprehensive. For several years my wife Emily and I lived in an apartment off Central Avenue near Briar Creek Road. Almost anything we needed was available on Independence. My employer, J.N. Pease, was located on East Independence, directly across from Ovens Auditorium. About everyone I knew was a customer of multiple retail establishments on Independence Boulevard The functionality of the boulevard to meet its design purpose became questionable when 70,000 vehicles a day passed by the Pease office. Local retail traffic and unlimited access finally forced the rebuilding of the roadway into a true freeway at a large cost and much inconvenience.

Independence: Drag Record 1 - 0

Independence had numerous traffic signals within its long straightaways

Ideal for street drag races. Not full-blown quarter mile runs but short blasts to satiate egos. Independence and Walnut (now named Freedom Drive) became a favorite location as there was clear sailing in either direction. The next intersection at Summit Avenue was also in play. Eastbound at Elizabeth and at The Plaza were favored locations. Police used "whammy's" then – two rubber tubes or hoses across travel lanes and they were connected to a timing device that registered speed. They could be easily spotted. Radar was out there but not likely to be encountered. With one exception, I abstained from such contests.

The exception occurred when I had a single lapse from the rigid discipline my father inculcated in me. Not long after graduation in early June 1963 my father traded our 1954 Ford for a 1961 Ford Galaxy Club Victoria (two door hardtop). It was black with red/white interior, had thick rocker panel chrome, power steering, power brakes, and AM radio all of which were extra cost at the time. It was slick and had a 352 cubic inch Ford "FE" V-8 that became a derated, middle engine option when the big 390 debuted in the fall of 1960. It was equipped with Ford's three speed Cruise-O-Matic transmission, two-barrel carburetor, and single exhaust good for 220 HP.

One evening James Sanders and I were cruising Independence from Bar-B-Que King to Shoney's on East Morehead (I usually avoided the Shoney's on East Independence – too far away and too much gas even at $0.32/gal). We came over the bridge by the pipe foundry in the inside lane (now West Carson Boulevard). The light at South Mint changed to red. I stopped. Next to me in the center lane was a 1955 Oldsmobile 88 coupe, I do not recall if it was a "Super 88" which often had the Olds 98 engine. In the curb lane was a 1962 Chevrolet Impala, I could see its "327" badge on the front fender just behind the headlights. We each knew what was about to go down. I thought the Chevy would win easily with its high revving small block although there was no way to externally distinguish a 250 horse from a very potent 300 horse 327 V-8. Did he have a four speed or the slush box two speed Powerglide? The Olds had some miles on it, but an '88 was no slouch. It no doubt had a GM Hydramatic transmission, the kind that seemed to keep shifting all the way into the next county. It would be a one-half block street run until it was time to slow for the South Church signal. If the Chevy had Powerglide it would be a close sprint. My Ford would come out first at 45, I would hold it for a second, and let up for the right-hand curve at Church Street. I figured if I stayed even with the Olds, I would be respectable as my Ford seemed especially fast and had more torque. James asked something like, "are you going?" "Yes," I responded.

The dealer had told my father the previous owner traveled often to Atlanta. Road cars were thought to be better than vehicles suffering from the daily stop and go of city driving. Unbeknownst to us, the previous owner wanted more power. He should have ordered 300 horsepower 390 Cu. In. V-8. He did the next best thing – found a capable mechanic who installed a compatible intake manifold for a four-barrel carburetor, perhaps a longer duration cam, I never knew. He did not add dual exhaust for an extra 10 horses but installed a large Carter AFB (which stood for aluminum four barrel).

The light changed and I put it on the floor. The four venturi's of the big Carter roared as they sucked in the air and suddenly there was no one beside me. James and I were astonished. In those few nanoseconds he called out that I had the Olds at least by one length and when my Ford upshifted, I backed off. The Chevy was third and that told me it was a 250 horse 327 with PowerGlide transmission which doomed his acceleration. The two vehicles passed me by with the Chevy's horses finally passing the Olds. I moved over to the curb lane; I had gotten by with it and it was time to quit. We wheeled into the Tops gas station located where the East Tower of Vantage South End exists today. Up went the hood. Blue valve covers and air filter housing meant it was indeed a 352. James spun the wing nut that held the air filter housing in place and took it off. There was a big Carter. What a surprise. I wisely (did not think so at the time) told my father about it and he had the engine restored to the factory's original equipment – a meager Ford two-barrel carb. Six decades later my drag record remains 1 – 0. And yes, it was good to shut down the Chevy.

Was There an Option?

There was a possible option. It would have required funding and more importantly a permission structure not extant at that time. Road building and improvements were widely viewed as progress, and little stood in their way. One possible alternative: Monroe Road might have been upgraded at the Rama-Monroe Road intersection. Then a Rama-Sardis-Fairview-Tyvola connector to US 74 might have been constructed using some of what is now the route of Woodlawn/Billy Graham Parkway. A circuitous, circumferential, and long-distance route that would require a lot of capital. Would there have been a commitment to build a road through the country/farmland to get around the city and one which would have failed to meet some of the Federal criteria?

Any viable option would need to stay within the basic constraints that were attached to the funding. Independence was designed with many acute shifts of its right of way; therefore, it is not far-fetched that a sky bridge from the sharp elevated curve over South Boulevard to the ridge line of the present East Third Street intersection with Carson Boulevard might have been considered.

That would have required the demolition of A.G. Junior High (which happened anyway after the 1958 school year), demolition of Kendall Mills offices on East Morehead, impacted several streets on the north side of Morehead, and likely crossed McDowell near the Domestic Laundry necessitating its demolition, and destroyed some of the easternmost streets of Brooklyn. The grade separation would have allowed the sky bridge to carry over the Thompson Orphanage pasture. A right-of-way for columns to support the bridge would have been required. There would have still been business and residential impacts and some costly rebuilding. Splitting Brooklyn would have been avoided. A smaller area would have been destroyed but not all of it. Urban renewal would have been based on other criteria. Impacts on the Elizabeth neighborhood would have still occurred unless the elevated roadway continued to intersect with the high bridge over the Seaboard Tracks. In the late 1940's, that was a bridge too far. Either option would likely have had unintended impacts to reinvestment and rehabilitation for Brooklyn. Surface streets support property development, and the political pressures would almost certainly have stopped either idea very quickly.

Chapter Notes

Urban Renewal: A default planning term used in the 1950s and 1960s for rehabilitation of declining areas of many US cities. In theory it was a tool that could regenerate cities. In some cases, it was necessary when neighborhood conditions became untenable. The term "slum" was a general moniker for a range of housing and or neighborhoods. The idea was to clear slums to create available land for newer, higher taxed development. It was intended that affected residents, most often renters, would be provided with new, presumably better housing elsewhere. Slum clearance was an objective of the Federal-Aid to Highway Act of 1944. Subsequently, many new highways including interstate system roads often obliterated lower income neighborhoods in many cities. The lower income and lesser valued "slums" were often occupied by Black and other minorities. New highways were needed in the post WWII era. In Charlotte, Earle Village was created for displaced residents from Brooklyn (Second Ward). Essentially a collection of multi-tenant blockhouse style brick dwellings that straddled East Seventh Street, Earle Village looked terrible when new and did not improve with time. There is still debate whether promises to those displaced were fulfilled. Presumably if something is bad enough to be replaced then the replacement itself should be crafted with contemporary standards of care. With the use of private sector financing Earle Village was demolished in the early 2000s and replaced by attractive contemporary apartments of various rent levels in the same general area.

J.N. Pease Associates: Leading architectural and engineering firm established in 1938 by Col. J. Normal Pease. Pease helped select Independence Boulevard's route through the city and created the first zoning map for the city in 1947. Known for its work with the US Army Corps of Engineers, Pease also designed Fort Bragg in 1940, hospitals, and water treatment facilities, including those in Charlotte. Pease designed notable buildings in Charlotte such as Knight Publishing (no longer extant), the Jefferson Standard Building at 301 South Tryon (now Wells Fargo), Jefferson First Union Tower at 300 South College (now Wells Fargo), and the Charlotte-Mecklenburg Government Center. In the 2010s Pease was purchased by La Bella and no longer exists as an entity. Pease was noted for its mentorship of younger architects, engineers, and technical designers. It was a superb environment in which to learn.

The big curve. Independence Blvd. at what is now East Brooklyn Village Avenue (formerly Stonewall Street). A cloudy winter day does nothing to warm this brutally vivid photo, showing an empty gasoline tanker heading west back to the Paw Creek terminal, clearly depicting how the boulevard sliced through the neighborhood. Note the power pole at the curb line, a perfect target for a vehicle long before seat belts were part of standard equipment. Photo: Robinson Spangler Carolina Room, Public Library of Charlotte- Mecklenburg County.

Independence Blvd. Viewed on a brighter day from East Morehead showing the big curve in the opposite direction. Directly ahead is the New Emmanuel Congregational Church. The 1951 Ford Victoria and the Biltmore Dairy (started at the George Vanderbilt estate – Biltmore – in Asheville) milk truck are using the short connector to South Caldwell Street as left turns were not possible at the big curve. The nearest vehicle is a 1953 Chevrolet. Two items of note: the large home on the right that would be razed in a few years; the post sign reading "Left Turns Keep Right". Photo: Robinson Spangler Carolina Room, Public Library of Charlotte-Mecklenburg County/J. N. Pease.

The bottom land. A photo from just west of Little Sugar Creek, this area was a pasture for Thompson Orphanage and was bisected by Independence Blvd. The Cherry community is ahead on the right in the tree line. Charlottetown Mall was later built just beyond the billboard, and the Charlottetown Twin Cinema was constructed on the left. The vehicle in the center is a 52 or 53 Oldsmobile so this was early in the boulevard's life. Photo: Robinson Spangler Carolina Room, Public Library of Charlotte- Mecklenburg County.

Contemporary view. The same view today with Belk Freeway Bridges passing over what is now East Brooklyn Village Avenue. The Metropolitan (building visible beyond overpass) resides on the site of the former Charlottetown Mall. Google photo.

Charlottetown Cinema. In late 1963 the twin screen Charlottetown Cinema opened opposite Charlottetown Mall. The theatre later became a four-screen house. Such notable films as "Thunderball" with Sean Connery and "Butch Cassidy and the Sundance Kid" were among its many features. It survived thirty years. Target now occupies the site. The early nineties skyline depicted here looks almost sparse compared to the 2020s. Photo: Author's collection.

1962 and 2024. East Independence and East Fourth Street. Fourth was still a two-way street and Independence was without turn lanes. Jerry's Drive later became the Athens 24-hour restaurant and lasted until the twenty-first century. The most current auto in view is a 1962 Chevrolet four door hardtop about to make a left turn from Fourth to East Independence. The home of author Harry Golden is on Elizabeth Avenue which is defined by the tree line beyond. Memorial Stadium is two blocks away on the left. This was once quiet Fox Street. Photo: Robinson Spangler Carolina Room, Public Library of Charlotte-Mecklenburg County.

CPCC Campus at Charlottetown Avenue (formerly Independence Blvd.) and East Fourth Street. Shaw Building stands where Jerry's Drive-In once resided. The original 1948/49 concrete is still in place at much of this location. Photo: Aurthor's collection.

Douglas and Sing Funeral Service. 1335 Elizabeth Avenue at Fox Street. This business was located at the corner of Elizabeth Avenue and Fox Street. Independence Blvd., now known as Charlottetown Avenue, shown in the previous photo, now travels directly over this property. Former Mayor Ben Douglas was one of its owners. Photo: Public Domain.

East Morehead /Independence Blvd./South Boulevard Intersection. This photo was taken behind the stairs shown in the photo on page 110. The western or phase two of Independence was some years away. The intersecting street on the right is South Boulevard. The vehicle that appears above the stair rail going from left to right is likely a 1953/54 Chevrolet. Three former homes front East Morehead in the distance. The residence on the corner was vacant but became the Coach Steak House for a year or two. Kuester's Dining Room is in the third dwelling behind the trees and near the South Caldwell intersection with Morehead. Photo: Robinson Spangler Carolina Room, Public Library of Charlotte-Mecklenburg County.

East Morehead/Independence/South Boulevard Intersection. A study in streetlight and traffic signal/signage technology of the times. In the center of the photo is A. G. Junior High School at 428 East Morehead. The Dowd YMCA stands there today. East Independence was completed at this intersection in 1949. The vehicles are all 1940s models and the nearest vehicle in the curb lane heading toward the school building is a 1949/50 Ford. A Duke Power GMC "old look" bus, No. 12 Route, East Morehead – Hutchinson Avenue was heading toward the Square. Photo: Robinson Spangler Carolina Room, Public Library of Charlotte-Mecklenburg County

East Morehead crossing South Blvd. – 2025. A close approximation of the previous photo. East Independence once connected to Morehead at grade at the heavy, broken line. There is complete grade separation now. Dowd YMCA is the building on the right at the former location of A. G. Junior High School. Google photo.

East Morehead /Independence/South Boulevard Intersection. Look carefully at this expanded view of the southwest corner of the city's most traveled intersection. Having just passed over the railroad bridge, there was a gasoline tanker pulled by a Mack tractor. Its driver would shortly turn left into Independence Blvd. and unlike previous years had a relatively unencumbered exit from the city. The tanker was one of many that moved gasoline from the Paw Creek terminal to points east of Charlotte. That function and the city's many trucking firms helped force the creation of Independence. The students were using one of the under-street crossings to reach A G Junior High School which stood on the southeast corner. A G closed following the 1957-58 school year and relocated. The Dowd YMCA was soon built and still resides there today. Photo: Robinson Spangler Carolina Room, Public Library of Charlotte- Mecklenburg County.

Another big curve. This 1972 photo shows Independence intact as completed 15 years previously (1957). The thoroughfare crossed South Tryon Street, then rose in elevation before making a ninety-degree left turn over South Blvd. and immediately dropped under East Moorehead. The onramp from South Blvd. would never be considered in today's engineering culture. Photo: Author's Collection.

Bill Lee Freeway. Interstate I-77. The Esso station at West Independence (now Wilkinson Blvd.) and Walnut Avenue (now Freedom Drive) about the early 1960s. The intersection was in a flat open area just north of the Southern Railway line embankment. Note the structure at the arrow which is barely visible on South Clarkson Street. Photo: Author's collection.

Bill Lee Freeway. Interstate 77. South Clarkson Street crosses over I-77 directly ahead and behind it is a bridge that carries the Norfolk Southern Railroad line over I-77. The barely visible structure at end of arrow can been seen in previous photo. Google photo.

Chapter 5
Airport and Environs

Douglas Municipal Airport

Ben Douglas Sr. was a mayor of Charlotte from 1935 -1941. His life and service to the city are well documented. Douglas was an advocate for the new Charlotte airport. Cannon Airport, which served as Charlotte's airport, was small and the surrounding topography made expansion problematic. The arrival of the Douglas DC-3 (no relation to Ben Douglas) in 1936 was a tectonic event for civilian air travel. Ben Douglas was an advocate for replacing Cannon with a new airport. DC-3s needed a field larger than Cannon. City bonds financed a new airport. Today the city's airport carries the former mayor's name. Douglas Municipal Airport became Charlotte Douglas International Airport in the early eighties.

The new Charlotte airport began in 1936. DC-3s entered airline service in 1936. It was the aircraft that established air travel as safe and comfortable. The new Charlotte field had its terminal building near the north end of runway 36 (now 36 R). The nearby hangar built by the WPA is still there but slightly relocated, restored, and part of the Sullenberger Aviation Museum. The weather bureau supposedly used the old terminal for a while before it was razed. It was gone by the 1960s by which time that end of the property was locally known as the "harbor lights". More on that later. Interestingly, there was a mobile home (trailer as they were known then) park between Wilkinson and Runway18, precisely where the beautifully lit parking garages are now. It must have been a noisy place to live. A fatal crash of an Air Force T-33 happened in the woods between the homes and the runway 18 South in early 1958.

During WWII Charlotte airport became a military training facility. Morris Field was named for an officer from Cabarrus County and was a training base for the US Army Air Forces. Its name is still in our lexicon. Into the seventies land surrounding the airport was still populated with former barracks-type buildings. Prior to 1954, when a new modern terminal building opened on the south side of the field between runways 18/36 and 5/23, passenger operations took place in a former Morris Field building close to the Air National Guard area. The runway and taxi lights were quite beautiful at night. When piston engine aircraft would take off to the north one could see blue flames of exhaust exiting their manifolds as they flew over the parking area. Those exhaust flames were powerful sensory stuff for an eight-year-old. After darkness fell a clinometer light would be visible piercing vertically to measure cloud ceiling.

A typical visit would begin after dinner, at least in warmer weather, when my father would drive from my grandmother's home on State Street, or later from our Kimberly Road home, out Wilkinson Blvd to Morris Field Drive which was populated with a small Black community around Plato Price School. Just before the turn off Wilkinson I could steal a brief glimpse of a movie at the South 29 Drive Theater. On warm evenings I enjoyed the cool breezes as Morris Field Drive traversed the woods where Billy Graham Parkway is today. Then up a slight grade and we would be there. Not in a forest but certainly in the countryside. There were a few homes on the left just before the airport.

A right turn just beyond the point where an Air Guard C-130 is presently displayed led us to the National Guard hanger and tarmac. Straight ahead was the terminal such as it was. It may have been the former base operations building. In fact, the airport perimeter abounded with buildings all of which had a "barracks style" architectural character. Turning left before the terminal would lead one past the airport fire department, down into a bottom and up a hill to West Blvd where Stonewall Jackson Homes were located.

The Terminals

At the terminal, there was a small area of parking against the fence that separated the aircraft gates from the parking area. The few lucky motorists who might arrive early enough could order curb service from the terminal restaurant. I had more than a few milkshakes there, usually brought to our car by a curb hop named "Willie". Sometimes we would exit our vehicle and stand at one of the loading gates which were simple openings in the chain link fence. There were always members of the military visible during the Korean War and WWII vets like my father (5th Air Depot Group, Eight Air Force) would readily engage in conversations with younger soldiers and airman.

On one such occasion my father began a conversation with a paratrooper awaiting a flight. I asked that young paratrooper what would happen if his chute did not open. He responded he would pull the rip cord on his reserve chute. Naturally, I asked what would happen if it also did not open. He responded that the Army would give him another one.

In those days (Korean War June 1950 – July 1953) I would see a lot of soldiers, especially uptown near the bus station. The paratroopers were always recognizable – trim and lean with their caps emblazoned with their airborne unit badges; their pants bloused and tucked into the tops their special boots. In a word they were cool.

Our visits satiated my need for sensory overload, both audible and visual. Those visits and my father's love of airplanes created a fascination with aviation. Between the terminal gates and the Guard hangar was a lineup of F-51Ds (formerly P-51Ds). A lot of F-51 units were called to active duty during Korea. The F-51s had replaced F-47Ds in the late forties. The 1948 film Fighter Squadron starting Robert Stack and Edmund O'Brien used F-47s in a starring role as 8th Air Force fighters. F-51s were used to represent German fighter aircraft. F-47s were scarce then so Guard units from several states contributed aircraft. NC Air Guard offered up four of its Thunderbolts to fill out the aircraft complement for filming. We did not own a camera, so I had no chance to photograph the beautiful B-26 Invader – AF serial 41-39327 - with its shark mouth nose art that reposed on the right side of the tarmac opposite the Guard hangar. It was used as a target tug for aerial gunnery practice and later in the fifties was acquired by the Chilean Air Force and based on available records was lost in a mid-air explosion in 1964.

Airline Operations

Charlotte was primarily an Eastern Airlines city. The airport was also served by Piedmont, and for a while Southern (much later a part of Republic). Capitol also stopped at Douglas, but I saw few of their aircraft until the British Vickers Viscounts arrived about 1957. Piedmont was a DC-3 outfit until the arrival of Fairchild F-27s (a license-built Fokker design) and surplus Eastern Martin 404s. Eastern used DC-3s, DC-4s, Martin 404s, and both L749 Constellations and L1049 Super Constellations, and later DC-7s.

The Martins were known as "Silver Falcons" and the Connies as "Golden Falcons". Early Connies had optional speed packs – large aluminum tubs that would attach to the ventral area between the main landing gears. They provided added package capacity, and it was fun to see them being attached to an aircraft.

Watching the airliners load and start engines was a surreal experience. Passengers of course walked to their planes and ascended exterior gangway steps – iffy in a rainstorm but the takeoff was likely delayed anyway. The gangways were often pushed by two ground personnel to and from the planes – being mounted on pickups came later.

My favorite event was watching the engines start. Starting a piston engine airliner is nothing like starting a modern jet airliner. First was the sound of an electric starter, the prop began to turn and turn faster followed by a coughing and belching of blue-white smoke of varying density. As the engine ran up RPMs the smoke slowly diminished and in short order there was a smooth mechanical sound, and another engine began the start procedure. Unlike modern jet engines, radial piston engines sometimes accumulate oil in their exhaust manifolds while sitting on the ramp, and occasionally the oil catches fire on startup. As each engine started, a groundcrew person would stand behind the engine with a large cart mounted fire extinguisher.

When a plane's flight engineer had all engines running smoothly and synced, the aircraft would rev up and with another groundcrew directing its pilot with those red-tipped flashlights I always desired. The plane slowly turned to starboard away from the gate as my father would hold onto his hat. For a short while we would smell exhaust blasts from burned 100+ octane aviation gasoline – and I enjoyed every second of it!

The ground vibrated and the prop sound was deafening standing only 100 feet away from four Wright R-3350 engines developing around 3,000 horses each. It was drama with precision and excitement.

The new 1954 terminal offered an observation deck with coin operated binoculars. A reasonable amenity to be sure. The new terminal offered upscale dining at the Airport 77 Restaurant. A fancy place indeed for this westside kid. I ate there only once when my father's sister and family were visiting. She had married a well-resourced gentleman – they had an air-conditioned auto even in 1956 - so they could afford to cover the meal. Yes,

Chapter 5 - Airport and Environs

I was easily impressed.

On a late afternoon in I believe 1962 my father drove us out to watch the first jetliner take off from Douglas. Based on the fleet roster, the first Eastern jets were Douglas DC-8-21s but the aircraft I saw takeoff, or so I recall, was a Boeing 720. We parked at the south end of the airport where NC 160 made a sharp curve. We watched the takeoff on Runway 23 as four early turbojets left smokey trails in the direction of Atlanta.

The other pathway to Douglas was West Blvd (New Dixie Road). Once past Remount Road the West Boulevard route quickly led into the hinterland of west Mecklenburg until one reached Jackson Homes. They were there in the middle of nowhere, having been built for officer housing in WWII. Beyond the airport were forests and fields all the way to the Catawba River. It was a terrific place to take a Sunday afternoon drive with my girlfriend once I had my driver's license. The lead-in road to the terminal was a T-intersection on West Blvd with the National Guard Armory residing on the right corner. Harding's 1963 prom took place in the armory on the evening of April 27, 1963. It was memorable because our chemistry/physics instructor, Mr. Eugene Todd, reportedly confiscated a small flask of bourbon from a classmate before its user could be seated. His name must remain redacted. Some distance away was a beach. Yes, a beach. Smitty's Beach was located on the east side of Wither's Cove bridge. Sand from the coast was placed to create a small beach area for visitors. Certainly not Myrtle Beach but a tolerable substitute for an afternoon of fun. Smitty's closed after the passing of its owner in the mid-sixties.

The entire area is hardly recognizable today although the 1954 terminal is still operating in a non-passenger capacity. In the early 1960s the airport extended Runway 18/36 from 5,000 to 7,500 feet. The soil necessary for filling the extension was excavated from the south side of West Boulevard, known at an earlier time as New Dixie Road. The location was directly opposite Jackson Homes. The large excavation soon became a dirt racetrack. The dust created by the races became a significant issue for its impact on the residents of the area. The track was defunct after a couple of years.

As time passed and the airport enlarged it created conflicts between the westside community and the airport. The area surrounding Douglas was rural and not populated by subdivisions as in the city limits. However, there were increasingly more residents there. One community was Moore's Park, located between US 29/74 and I-85, and a short distance west of Little Rock Road. Few people would have anticipated back in the 1950s and early 1960s the exponential growth of Douglas International Airport. In the nineties Moore's Park and homes in other impacted communities were acquired, and residents relocated via the Federal Part 150 Program.

Depending on an aircraft's flight path and the TV signal direction, television interference might be minor to terrible. It was especially bad when "rabbit ear" interior antennas were in use. When a TV screen was filled with specks, we called it snow. A TV picture screen with undiscernible lines at forty-fives degrees from vertical and rapidly moving, indicated an airliner was about to fly over one's home. The interference we accepted as troubling is unheard of with modern means of signal delivery. Unlike later jet airliners, prop aircraft were easily distinguishable even from within one's home. The audible signature of a DC-3 was automatic, DC-4s similar but stronger. Martin 404s had their own acoustic signature. Constellations and later DC-7s were louder and had a throatier sound with their bigger Wright engines.

Jets were on the way. Eastern DC-7s would be gone by 1966 and the Connies by 1968. Early jets were noise and smoke producers by virtue of their straight turbo jet engines. By the time I graduated from Harding, Eastern Airlines already had a fleet of forty Lockheed L-188 Electra prop jets which were quieter than pure jets. While newer jet airliners began to use early "turbofan engines" that were less noisy, impacts to westside neighborhoods remained a significant issue. Today there are specific FAA requirements for various classifications of planes and aircraft are indeed much quieter. Growing up, we simply accepted it as part of living on the westside.

My most memorable experiences happened whenever a flight of four F-51Ds streaked over my grandmother's house at 1108 State Street. F-51s equipped the Air National Guard until F-86As withdrawn from Korea replaced them. On weekends when the Guard might be flying and if a southerly wind were blowing, they would fly directly over my grandmother's house, throttle back on power, and peel off for their base leg for final approach to runway 23. The Mustang became the iconic fighter aircraft of WWII once its Allison V12 power plant was replaced with Rolls Royce Merlin liquid cooled V-12s. Packard Motor Company built the Merlin engines under license. There are few mechanical sounds more mellifluous than four F-51s backing down as they streaked overhead. I could hear them coming and knew I had only a few seconds to reach my grandmother's backyard to see them blast over casting their melodious wail.

The F-86As gave way to F-86Ls whose afterburner flames were neat to see on takeoff. The father of my friend and classmate Bobby Brooks was the squadron commander for the Guard. By the early sixties the Air Guard became a transport unit. They went through C-119s, C-121s, and operated the big Douglas C-124 Globemaster for some years. Ironically, they now operate C-17 Globemaster IIs.

On a summer evening in my senior year in high school two friends and I drove to the still modern terminal. I had only recently obtained my driver's license and was driving my father's 1954 Ford. One of my friends was a student civilian pilot. We walked out the north concourse – one of three at the terminal - and there sat a Delta DC-7B laying over the night for a return flight to Atlanta early the next day. We simply walked up the stairs onto the plane – the first time I had been in an airplane. A maintenance guy soon emerged from the cockpit and told us we should leave but he was pleasant about it.

Back in the terminal, we walked up the interior stairs to the control tower and knocked on the door. We noticed a small peep tube in the door as we heard a voice asking what we wanted. My friend told the voice he was a student pilot – he and his friends were just looking around – TSA are you listening? He opened the door and let us in to observe the operations. Nothing ventured, nothing gained. Thirty years later I made it into the tower legitimately as Chairman of the City's Airport Advisory Committee.

Chapter Notes

Ben Douglas Sr.: Douglas was a three-time Charlotte mayor (1935-1941), businessman, and leading advocate for civic development. Charlotte benefited from federal programs during the Great Depression. New Deal dollars flowed to the city to build Memorial Stadium, Charlotte Memorial Hospital (now Atrium), and the first subsidized public housing for both White people and for Black people. Douglas Municipal Airport was named in his honor. Following his terms as mayor he actively sought funding for a cross-town major road that became Independence Boulevard

Turbojets/Turboprops: Post WWII era US airliners were powered by air cooled radial piston engines. Some of these powerplants pushed piston engine technology to its limits. Great Britain put the first jet powered airline in service in 1952. A series of crashes due to pressurization failures forced the withdrawal of the British Comet airliner. The first US jet powered airliner, the Boeing 707, made its first scheduled flight on October 26, 1958, a Pan Am route from New York to Paris. American Airlines inaugurated the first domestic service in January 1959. Early jetliners were powered with turbojet engines which used a compressor section to compress air and feed it into burners where it was combusted, the exhaust gases of which turned an exhaust turbine connected to the central engine shaft connected to the compressor. These engines were noisy and smokey. By the early 1960s the first generation of turbofan engines were introduced. They were quieter and more fuel efficient. Turboprops were a hybrid design in which a jet engine powered a conventional propeller. They produced less power but were quieter and more fuel efficient than turbojets. In many route applications turboprop aircraft were as useful as jet airliners. Many smaller airliners were turboprop powered as were some important military aircraft. Contemporary Stage 3 engines are of very large diameter and produce high levels of thrust but with much quieter operation. Turboprop powered aircraft are still used today.

F-86A/F-86L: The F-86 Sabre or Sabre Jet was the first US sweep wing jet fighter (term used before being corrupted to fighter jet). It was built by North American Aviation Company, builder of the famed WWII P-51 (later F-51) Mustang. The aircraft was based on captured German engineering documents that were returned to the US after WWII. Turns out the Soviet Union likewise collected German aeronautical data and built the Mikoyan Gurevich MiG-15. MiG-15s were introduced early in the Korean War and outclassed all UN straight wing fighters. The only western aircraft capable of fighting MiG-15s on equal terms was the F-86. The F-86A model was successively replaced by the "E" and "F" models as the war progressed. About 1954/55 NC Air Guard in Charlotte, 156th Fighter Interceptor Squadron, received F-86As that had been replaced in front line service. They served in the air defense role flying out of Douglas Municipal Airport. By 1959 a dedicated radar equipped interceptor version of the Sabre, the F-86L (modified F-86Ds and equipped with a retractable tray of aerial rockets), began replacing the older F-86As and served until the Air Guard transitioned to a military airlift mission with transport aircraft.

Douglas Municipal Airport. Passenger terminal prior to 1955. This is part of a long linear building that is almost certainly a base operations facility from the WWII era Morris Field. Several views of this structure exist and have been dated to 1960 which was after a new modern terminal on the airport's south side between runways 5-23 and 18-36 opened in 1954. This building was at the very end of Morris Field Drive. There were parking spaces at the opposite end of the building (on left out of photo) where locals might park and watch planes load and unload. Photo: Used with permission of J. Murrey Atkins Library, University of North Carolina at Charlotte.

Ready to taxi. Its four Pratt and Whitney R-2000 engines running smoothly, this bird is ready to turn right and depart the gate. Just to the left of the ground crewman and under the aircraft can be seen the 1937 hangar at the north end of runway 18-36. The hangar has been modernized and is now a part of the Sullenberger Aviation Museum, albeit it has been slightly relocated. A facsimile of a DC-4 graced the 1946 US Postal airmail stamp. Photo: Courtesy C. Jack Washam III.

Douglas Municipal Airport Terminal. This is the terminal as it appeared from the end of WWII until the new terminal opened in 1954. Openings for the gates were on the chain link fence on the right. The hangar and water tower in the background were part of the Morris Field WWII complex. A large tarmac area was beyond the water tower, and the flight line for fighter planes was behind the Eastern Airlines DC-3 (no fighter aircraft in this photo). Photo: Courtesy C. Jack Washam III.

Douglas DC-4 loading. In the background is a Douglas DC-3, the first truly modern airliner. DC-3s first flew in 1936 and continued in airline service into the early 1960s. Over 10,000 military C-47 versions were built in WWII. It was slow and not pressurized so it flew low. Developed prior to tricycle landing gear technology, it was a tail sitter. The DC-4 was the next model from Douglas. Most used by airlines were taken from some 500 surplus craft following the war. Also unpressurized, it carried 44 +/- passengers, was faster and flew higher with greater range. Eastern Airlines had nearly 40 and flew then until about 1960. In the 1950s DC-6s and Lockheed Constellations became the heavy haulers for Eastern. Photo: Courtesy C. Jack Washam III.

1954 Terminal. This post card photo depicts the 1954 (some sources state early 1955) terminal essentially as originally constructed and prior to late 1960s additions. Three Eastern Airlines Lockheed Electras in the intermediate paint scheme prior to the hockey stick livery of 1964 date this photo to be early 1960s. Eastern had gates on the west side of the north concourse and the entire west concourse. Delta, Piedmont, Southern, and Capital were handled at the remaining gates although Delta's late afternoon flight to Atlanta, a stretch DC-8-61, typically used the end of the north concourse. This distribution later changed in the 1970s when Delta and especially Piedmont begin increasing their numbers of flights. When Piedmont declared Charlotte a hub in 1979 flights increased dramatically. By the spring of 1981, in what looked like a row of jet bombers, Piedmont would line up 10 -12 Boeing 737-200s by 8:00 AM just to the east of the north concourse. Photo: Robinson-Spangler Carolina Room, Public Library of Charlotte-Mecklenburg County.

1954 Terminal. The best photos of the then new terminal were part of this post card showing front and rear elevations including the starboard side of an Eastern Airline Super Constellation. The first vehicle in the line of parked vehicles is a 1956 Oldsmobile 98, so these images likely represent 1956/1957. Inside was the popular Airport 77 Restaurant. an observation deck on the concourse side provided, binocular viewing as visiting the airport to see airliners loading, taking off, and landing was a popular weekend activity. The terminal served ever growing air traffic until the newer and present terminal opened on April 18, 1982. The 1954 structure still exists and has been repurposed. Photo: Robinson Spangler Carolina Room, Public Library of Charlotte-Mecklenburg County.

Flagship Wilkes Barre. American Airlines (the original, one of the big four) served Charlotte for a while. Several airlines, and notably Piedmont of the 1970/80s, gave names to their aircraft. This is a DC-6B reposed on the east side of the north concourse at the 1954 terminal. This was four years before the southern extension of runway 18L- 36R and a tree is visible in the background. Eastern was the dominant carrier at Douglas in the fifties. Piedmont, Capital, and Southern each served the city but with far fewer flights. Author's collection.

NC National Guard flight line at Douglas Municipal Airport. The lineup is: four F-47D Thunderbolts, two T-6 Texans, and one B-26C Invader used for target towing. This is the only B-26 the guard had and the one I remember although it did not yet have its shark nose paint. The F-47s (P prefix was changed to F in 1947) were superseded by F-51Ds. The F-47D Thunderbolt was known as "The Jug" in WWII and was designed by noted immigrant engineer Alexander Kartveli. One or more of these Thunderbolts might have participated in the 1948 film "Twelve O'clock High". The National Guard area was at the end of Morris Field Drive and to the right or north of the pre-1954 terminal building, essentially where it is today. Photo: Courtesy NC Air Guard.

Flight Line. The Air Guard, 156th Fighter Squadron, F-51s were replaced by F-86A jet fighters which provided air defense for North and South Carolina. Sometime in late 1958 or early 1959 more modern radar equipped F-86L interceptors arrived to equip the squadron. They were armed with 24 - 2.75-inch folding fin rockets within a retractable weapons tray under the cockpit. This photo, taken under a leaden sky with my Brownie Hawkeye, was at an open house probably in February 1959. It depicts the flight line showing two of the squadron's shiny and recently acquired F-86Ls. Photo: Author's collection.

601 West Trade - 1962. Southern Railway Depot resided on Southern's Washington – New Orleans main rail line. The city's overwhelming volume of rail passengers traveled through the 60-year-old station. It also handled passenger trains from the Columbia Division and Mooresville-Statesville (until 1951). The photo was dated 1962 and indeed the vehicle in the center is a 1962 Pontiac Star Chief sedan. A grade separation project in the early 1960s relocated the tracks over West Trade and West Fourth Streets, the Depot being razed in the process. It was replaced by a new but small station on North Tryon Street. Photo: Robinson Spangler Carolina Room, Public Library of Charlotte- Mecklenburg County.

601 West Trade - 2025. This photo shows the roof of the Greyhound Bus Station at the left, streetcar tracks on a median divided West Trade Street, and the Norfolk Southern mainline tracks passing over Trade. The city's new intermodal passenger station will be constructed at this location. Google photo.

Chapter 6
Trains, Buses, and Cabs – But No Boats

Steel Rails – Southern Railway

Charlotte is not defined by proximity to a large river or navigable waterway.

Commerce and passenger travel before the era of modern aviation was via train, bus, and by motor carrier trucks. In the nineteenth century the port of Charleston could be reached by rail from Charlotte. Four railroads, three of which exist today — Southern Railway, Seaboard Airline Railroad, Norfolk Southern (original), and Piedmont and Northern served Charlotte, Southern Railway's main line from Washington ran through Charlotte on its way to Atlanta and New Orleans. It also had a line to Columbia from Charlotte. Southern is now Norfolk Southern (after its 1982 merger with Norfolk Western) and its line through the city is serious railroading.

The Southern 1900s era station resided on West Trade where the Greyhound station stands today. Southern had a brick office building adjacent to its coach yard, opposite the station and across the main line. The grade crossing necessitated a gate tower with a gate man who manually controlled the crossing gates. West Trade vehicular traffic sometimes backed up following passage of a long freight. It was with anticipation that I looked in both directions when the Green Street bus crossed the tracks, always in hopes of seeing a headlight in the distance. It was nothing short of spellbinding to gaze at two ribbons of steel and imagine what unusual locomotives and cars might be heading my way. Even today seeing a loco headlight in the distance is mesmerizing.

Southern had a secondary line to Mooresville and Statesville where it connected with its Salisbury/Asheville line. Its Columbia division funneled trains from Augusta and Columbia to Charlotte. Southern had a large yard, engine facilities, and a turntable parallel to North Tryon beginning at 16th Street. The present 1960s era Amtrak station (formerly Southern) is located near 23rd Street on North Tryon and much of the Southern yard is adjacent to it. Here Southern interchanged freight with both the original Norfolk Southern and Seaboard. It also blocked freight cars originating from

Charlotte. The original Norfolk Southern trackage to mid-North Carolina is now a successful short line - Aberdeen Carolina and Western. NS was acquired by Southern in 1974 and later sold to a smaller operator.

On warm evenings my father would drive us to the Southern Depot (an older term for stations) and we would watch the Southern Crescent arrive from New Orleans. Virtually all premiere and first-class trains had names. It typically was headed by several twin diesel 2900 series EMD (General Motors) E-6 locomotives in green and white with gold striping – the classic Southern colors. The Charles R. Jonas Federal Court House at Mint and Trade, site of the original Charlotte Mint, was also the main Post Office at the time. Fourth Street was not continuous with its western segment and terminated at the tracks. Railroads held government mail contracts until 1967, so in the fifties most mail except more expensive air mail moved by rail, mostly via passenger trains. It was only a block from the depot and therefore, quite convenient for loading mail into mail or baggage express rail cars on a station rail siding. For many decades Railway Express Agency (REA) carried a huge share of packages. REA became defunct in the 1970s as UPS and FedEx became dominant. Passenger trains declined following cancellation of mail contracts since mail was the revenue source that kept many passenger trains in service. Amtrak took over in 1971.

Typically the locomotives of north bound passenger trains would uncouple, cross West Trade and back up to couple onto mail and express cars, and possibly a Pullman sleeper, prepositioned in the coach yard. The locos then reversed the movement and recoupled to the train consist. Once the additional cars were coupled on and a test of its brake line made, the streamliner, which usually had all fluted, stainless-steel cars would rev up and slowly begin to move. The concrete paving resonated from the combustion of 6,000 horsepower —six diesel prime movers in three locomotives. When the dining car passed, I could see passengers enjoying dinner. On warm humid evenings there would be condensate around the edges of the large windows. Real class I thought. It helped create a love of trains that still resides within me.

But wait! I saw another headlight. A freight train? No, another passenger train entering the main (primary track) from Graham Street. Not a premier train but a second-class train, perhaps from Columbia/Augusta? This was

Chapter 6 - Trains, Buses, and Cabs — But No Boats

good news as we would stay until it pulled in and stopped at the depot. How did this happen, how did the train reach the depot?

The answer is a forgotten circuitous cross over from the Columbia Division track that ran straight through the heart of downtown. The Columbia tracks transited Pineville and paralleled South Boulevard. There were carload customers in what we now call "The South End" and at one time a small yard just south of Tremont Avenue existed to store rail cars. The line continued parallel to Tryon Street, from East Hill Street to East Fourth Street a large multi-track yard serviced the Southern freight station. Before trucks captured LCL (less than carload) business, rail freight terminals operated like trucking terminals by transloading from rail to local delivery truck. The line continued north with storage tracks north of East Fifth and East Sixth Streets, then crossed/interchanged with the Seaboard line near the Seaboard station and entered the primary Southern yard.

Passenger trains used a different route to reach the Southern Depot. They entered a left-hand switch just after passing under East Morehead Street. Then via an embankment behind the Querry Spivey McGee feed and seed store which occupied the corner of Stonewall and College, continued by what once was a Goodyear Store (now Ally Bank), and crossed South Tryon, and then went westward just south of the original Observer Building. South The track continued as Church Street rose over the tracks on an old-style arch bridge, then ducked behind the M&T snack plant and onward to cross South Mint a little north of Good Samaritan Hospital. The track then turned northward and crossed over South Graham to travel behind Atlantic Beer after which it entered the Southern main line just south of the depot. The only vestige remaining to define the route is a concrete abutment (west side of South Mint Street) on which rested one end of the plate girders of the deck girder bridge that spanned the street. Part of the embankment behind the Goodyear Store was discernible until obliterated with new construction.

For many years the Charlotte Christmas Parade began at South-East-West Boulevards, thence to East Morehead where it turned left, then turned right onto Tryon until it ended at the Sears parking lot at Tryon and Eleventh Streets. I recall one year a passenger train arrived during the parade. It stopped at South Tryon and waited. The parade units continued to cross the tracks. Its engineer sounded the horn and the diesels began moving, the parade had to momentarily stop. The train arrived at the depot on time.

Only a few passenger trains crossed South Tryon each day. The larger issue was long freight trains that could block West Boulevard, West Park Avenue, and streets north of Trade Street. About 1954 Southern constructed a cut off that veered westward at a point just south of present Tyvola Road, skirted the Billy Graham Museum property, and entered the mail line just west of Old Steel Creek Road near Wilkinson Boulevard It still whisks heavy Norfolk Southern traffic onto and from the Columbia line.

As it turned out in June of 1954 Southern's two block long uptown freight terminal, loaded with merchandise, burned to destruction in one of the city's largest fires. My friends and I could hear sirens all around. Southern and local merchants took a heavy hit because of the losses. Southern did not rebuild the terminal. The Columbia division tracks continued to move local traffic until the mid/late-1980s. The north-south Lynx Blue Line opened in 2006 and operates on the same right-of-way, but not the same track infrastructure, that once carried Southern freight traffic. The remaining original Columbia division tracks stop now at the ADM plant on South Boulevard

In the early 1960's a major grade separation project was begun that raised the Southern mainline over Trade, Fourth (now continuous to Cedar Street), and Fifth Streets. Southern relocated its station – now Amtrak - to a smaller facility on North Tryon Street. Southern did not join Amtrak in 1971 but finally did so in 1979. Eventually Amtrak will serve a planned multi-modal terminal on the site of the original Southern Depot.

Seaboard Airline Railroad

Seaboard, now part of CSX, was and is the city's east-west railroad. The term "airline" was intended to mean straight as going through the air. It was a north-south line undulating through the Sand Hills from Richmond to Florida. Its western mainline ran from its big Hamlet hub through Waxhaw onto Atlanta and Birmingham. At Monroe the Charlotte sub-division peels off and continues to Charlotte, thence to Rutherfordton. There it connects with the former Clinchfield line (now CSX) at nearby Bostic. Its Charlotte yard and terminal are adjacent to Rozzells Ferry Road between Hoskins and Hovis Roads. It was and still is a very good photo spot for rail fans. A smaller yard existed partially on and just west of the overpass bridge over North

Chapter 6 - Trains, Buses, and Cabs – But No Boats

Tryon.

Seaboard had a few shippers in the Central Avenue area and in the sixties/seventies serviced the concrete batch plant formerly at the McAlway Road crossing. It served as a bridge line between Tennessee/Kentucky and the southeast, becoming a heavy coal line in the 1970s through 2015. Daily freight trains still connect Hamlet with Eastman Chemical in Kingsport TN. Grain trains from the Midwest sometimes transit Charlotte on their way to the coastal ports. I liked Seaboard's locomotive livery. I could get a glimpse of their locos and rolling stock when my father's bus went under the Seaboard overpass on North Tryon. Seaboard interchanged with Southern just east of the Seaboard's North Tryon station. For the most part however, Seaboard was out of sight and out of mind.

Seaboard offered one daily train each way between Wilmington and Rutherfordton (in the fifties it was cut back to Wilmington – Charlotte, Nos. 13 and 14)). Unfortunately, I never saw either one. Matthews and the general store at Rama Road crossing were rural flag stop stations. The downtown station was on the track level which was above Tryon Street grade. The building survives. The final run to Wilmington was late in 1958 – a photo opportunity that was missed, even with my Brownie Hawkeye. Seaboard and Atlantic Coast Line merged in 1967 to become Seaboard Coast Line, later to become Seaboard System. After merging with Chessie System the new entity became CSX. Norfolk Southern and CSX later acquired and then split Conrail - the result of the highly successful 1976 Federal assumption of bankrupt northeast railroads.

Norfolk Southern - The Original

NS was a single-track freight line from Norfolk to Charlotte via Raleigh. It was a bridge line that also serviced quarries, timber lands, and the rich farming areas in the eastern center of the state. It was a favorite of rail fans in part because of their vermillion Baldwin locos with black striping. The line entered the city from the east, crossed Sharon Amity as it still does, then crossed east 36th Street and paralleled North Brevard Street. A small brick building served as its terminal where it interchanged with Southern.

There was no way for me to see any activity since their yard, even from a city bus window, was mostly above street grade. Something I wanted but could not have and it was much too far to reach by walking. It eluded my quest, and it was not until 1972 that I finally photographed a couple of locomotives. NS was acquired by Southern in 1974, its locomotives were repainted, and its identity lost. The newer Norfolk Southern later shed the line, which is doing quite well now as the Aberdeen, Carolina and Western with Charlotte being its western terminus. It is headquartered in Candor where it serves the largest chicken feed plant in the world.

Piedmont and Northern

If Seaboard and Norfolk Southern were elusive, then P&N would be ubiquitous on the west side of the city. It was created in the 1910s by Duke Power Company and intended to be a catalyst for industrial growth. It had two disconnected divisions: Charlotte-Mt Holly-Gastonia; Spartanburg-Greenville-Anderson-Greenwood in South Carolina. Duke's attempt to get ICC approval to connect the two was successfully opposed (politically lobbied) by Southern. Several of its signature stations still exist, and one is visible between Old Mt Holly Road and Moore's Chapel Road intersection.

P&N was electrically powered from overhead catenary lines and hauled regular merchandise freight and heavy coal trains to Duke power plants. It also provided passenger service with "interurban" cars. The powered units were passenger cars with self-contained electric motors on the driving axles. Interurban service, popular in many metropolitan locations, was a convenient way to travel from the Gastonia area to Charlotte and return. In 1951 passenger service ended, which was likely caused by proliferation of autos. P&N soon went to all diesel locomotive roster and the high maintenance overhead wires came down. Six Alco S-4 switchers served Charlotte. P&N's main yard and maintenance facility at Pinoca was adjacent to the Seaboard yard along Rozzells Ferry Road

The story of P&N is something of a narrative of the city's west side in the twentieth century. Its tracks, some still under soil or pavement of new parking lots, saturated the area west of South Mint Street and between the West Morehead corridor and Stewart Creek. From there it went directly to its Pinoca yard, crossed the Catawba River rail bridge and then into Mt Holly and to Gastonia.

Its Charlotte passenger terminal was located on precisely the land

Chapter 6 – Trains, Buses, and Cabs – But No Boats

occupied by Truist Field. The passenger station was set in a corner framed by West 4th and South Mint and outside the park and in line with center field, The freight station was sited approximately at the main entrance to the ball field.

A large yard was nestled between Mint and Graham Streets, the tracks of which crossed 2nd and 3rd Streets at grade. At this yard P&N classified trains going to their west yard at Pinoca and serviced the Chesapeake Paper building at 3rd and Graham. Warehoused there were paper products including newspaper print paper. Rumor was that it had a 200 lb./sq ft live load rating so its concrete floors could carry the weight of heavy rolls of paper. To service the Swift & Company meat distribution facility nearby, P&N did "street running" in the middle of Mint Street. In fact, its electric locos were used for that purpose until 1958, thereby becoming the last catenary powered freight locomotives in Charlotte.

The entry to the Mint Street yard was via lead tracks from the Cedar Street yard which ran under both the Southern station tracks from the Columbia Division, the path of which is no longer visible, and its Washington-Atlanta mainline. The upper Cedar Street yard still has a small amount of trackage which is directly adjacent to the Charlotte Rescue Mission. F&R Coal & Oil at 624 South Cedar was a customer of P&N. There was still a demand through the 1950s for coal as a heating fuel, and I was fascinated seeing coal cars (hoppers) unloading from the lower tracks into storage bins. The two uptown yards stored inbound/outbound loads and empties.

Its customer base was the many machine shops, manufacturing shops of various kinds, and storage buildings for all sorts of things that dotted the area. Spur tracks radiated to Elliott Street where old maps indicate P&N had an interchange with Southern in the vicinity of Charlotte Pipe and Foundry. Tracks then crossed Morehead just west of today's I-77 and found their way to the Bryant Street area and eventually looped over Thrift Road and onto the "main line" near Tuckasegee Road. It was from this loop a spur led to the new A&P warehouse at 2024 Thrift Road, now apartment buildings. A separate spur left the main north of its State Street Crossing them paralleled Berryhill Road, then crossed Thrift Road to service several customers, including General Electric, and Rulane Propane Gas (later and presently Suburban Propane). Often at night when at my grandmother's I would hear the chirping of ALCO S-4 diesel turbochargers as P&N switched the GE repair shop at Tuckasegee and Thrift Roads.

The line bisected Wesley Heights by crossing Summit Avenue, Grandin Road and Walnut Avenue on its way west. Tracks no longer exist between downtown and Pinoca. Decades ago, P&N crossed Parkway Avenue at Norwood, the site of a Duke Power substation. In the western corner of the juncture was Lakewood Park and Pavilion, a recreation venue and subject for a post card illustration. P&N was a convenient way to get there for a day of family fun. A corn field occupied the lake bottom when I first saw the site about 6 years of age. The pavilion was long gone. One could also transfer between P&N and Duke Power bus service where the tracks crossed Hoskins Road. A mile westward P&N interchanged with Seaboard where their respective yards joined west of Hoskins along Rozzells Ferry. P&N conveniently served a 1950s industrial park nearby on Hovis Road.

I was visiting a client, Melvin Carson, at Duke Power when I last saw a Seaboard Coast Line switcher at the Mint Street yard in 1978 or 79. With no cell phone and no camera, the moment was lost. Interestingly, to celebrate the nation's bi-centennial in 1976 several class 1 railroads each painted a locomotive in special bi-centennial liveries. Seaboard's "1776" was probably the most notable of that group. In the summer of 1976, it was reposed, replete with martial music and flags, in the Mint Street yard and I drove uptown for a look, but without our little Kodak Instamatic. It was a GE U-36B, a 3,600 HP freight road loco and no doubt the largest loco to every visit the P&N. The last customer was likely a chemical plant to the left of Alfred Williams (Klingman Williams then) warehouse located on Freedom Drive. In the early 2000s, a friend photographed a couple of CSX GP-40s from Pinoca serving the plant by using a switch back located in the bottom land of Stewart Creek just west of West Morehead near Freedom Drive.

P&N was a well-managed railroad with a low operating ratio. It remained profitable and was sold to Seaboard Coast Line (a merger of Atlantic Coast Line and Seaboard Airline) in 1969. In our urban environment where trucks are everywhere, it may be difficult to visualize the volume of railroad freight cars that dotted the city into the fifties. For kids there was something interesting to discover around every corner. I sought freight cars of railroads far away as it was fun, something like looking for the most distant vehicle

Chapter 6 – Trains, Buses, and Cabs – But No Boats

license plate. In a significant geographical area of the city people and their residences co-existed with a railroad. Perfect for a railroad guy like me. Today rail traffic is concentrated in intermodal, aggregates, grain, lumber. The single car business still exists but not in central Charlotte.

Buses – Duke Power/City Coach Lines

Through most of my childhood transit buses were an essential component of city life. Charlotte relied on streetcars until 1938 when the system operator, Duke Power Company, effected a complete switch to buses that had started in 1934. My father began diving for Duke in 1939. I was born long after the streetcars departed our city streets.

Like its railroad, P&N, Duke Power streetcars ran on electrical power. Streetcars are cleaner, require less upkeep, need no tires, and are quieter. Unlike trolley buses they cannot deviate from their catenaries that are expensive to install. Streetcars and light rail can be quite efficient in dense urban applications. Buses provide flexibility and can quickly move onto new routes to accommodate new residential growth. They of course require fuel even with hybrid designs.

A Charlotte map of 1935 looks much like one from 1950. Duke's 1949 routes were extensive and managed to cover the city rather well geographically. Until I was married I lived no more than a few blocks from bus transportation and for many years buses traveled the streets where I lived. I overheard my father, a career bus driver, comment during a discussion that between 1950 and 1955 ridership increased, and between 1955 and 1960 it diminished. If we look at route maps of the late 1950s, we see longer routes as the bus system expanded to serve residential growth, especially on the east and south sides.

Duke ran bus systems for nine cities in the Carolinas. Duke sold its Charlotte operation to City Coach Lines in 1955. Buses seemingly forever had advertisements on their ceilings above the standee windows. To optimize income potential, they would soon carry external placards for advertisers. Transit service was not a big profit operation and often lost money. Transit buses were an economic necessity to move people to and from employment. In a way, they were lubricant that helped keep our local economy functioning efficiently.

GMC (General Motors Coach) was the predominate coach maker and so City Coach standardized with GMC buses. Duke had stabled several manufacturers which complicated maintenance. The remaining Ford coaches – handy smaller buses - were soon gone. City Coach quickly acquired new GMC 35-foot air ride coaches 1021 through 1034. The tops of each side carried the script logo "New GM Air Ride Coach" to entice ridership. (A similar market strategy was used in 1978 when Charlotte Transit used 25 new design GMC RTS models to increase ridership). The ridership was still heavy and 1021 through 1034 were 41 passenger configurations rather than 45 as the first four rows on the driver side were single seats. But why have fewer seats? Simple, to have more room for standees in busy "peak hour" service periods.

City Coach made operational changes. It was trying to be successful in a marginal business and each dime counted. Duke's open, unsecured fareboxes were replaced with secured boxes that were opened by designated employees at the end of the day. Drivers entered passenger loads on forms that were turned in following their shifts. City Coach installed pole mounted phones at each end of its routes. Each driver was supplied with $100 in operating change. Random checks were made in the drivers' ready room to ensure no one had made a loan to himself.

In hindsight it is remarkable how frequently buses ran their routes during that time. Lighter routes such as #2 Green Street- Oakhurst (later Coliseum) ran a 30 minute off peak headway, 20 during peak. Route #4 Park Road- Belmont ran 15 minutes during peak and had an alternate route at peak hours only with 15 a minute's headway. Peak hours effectively ran 6:30 – 9:30 a.m., and 3:30 – 7:00 p.m. This meant some drivers would have a split shift doing only peak service. Others had either an "day shifts" or "late straight shifts". The years we did not have a car, my father preferred a "swing shift" – between peak hours so he could ride our local route to and from work.

Drivers would bid on routes via a seniority system. Each route pivoted about the Square as its central transfer point. Every route had an out and back to each side for a total trip. For my detail-oriented mind, the route system was fascinating. Each day each first shift driver would start his assigned bus at the bus garage and then position his bus at the Square at

Chapter 6 - Trains, Buses, and Cabs – But No Boats

the prescribed starting time so his position in the racetrack pattern would be correct. Remarkably, City Coach followed Duke's operational procedure, and every driver would drive the same bus every day except for maintenance downtime. So, if I rode the #2 bus downtown each day at 9:30 a.m. I would ride perhaps 849. Remarkable discipline and order.

The application of equipment by City Coach reflected societal demographics as it had with Duke. In the 1950s Black neighborhoods were heavily dependent on public transit and subsequently ridership on the "Black routes" was higher during almost all hours. Duke's first 35-foot 45 passenger coaches, 891 through 897; 912, 913, were assigned to #16 York Road-Double Oaks, No. 2 Biddleville-Second Ward. My father preferred newer equipment and was willing to bid for higher density routes to have a new bus. Soon after the sale to City Coach 1001 through 1013 arrived and these big guys met the maximum width allowed by law of 102 inches instead of the usual 96 inches. They had 51 seats and were 40-foot coaches. They were more tedious to drive on any street and especially through the narrow confines of Brooklyn (Second Ward). My father had little difficulty getting a winning bid on Route #7 and drove 1002. At the time I did not know that the father of my friend John Vann had a grocery store nearby at 427 South McDowell Street very close to Route #7 which I rode many times.

Another example was the #3 Oaklawn-Selwyn Avenue service. Oaklawn was a Black community. Selwyn Avenue bisected the Queens Road area and was White and affluent, or upscale as we would say now. Domestic workers – maids or housekeepers as they were called – might live in the Oaklawn area and have employment in the Selwyn area and if so, could travel directly to their place of work without transferring. My father drove No. 3 in 1958/59. I recall one day before going home, I rode out Selwyn with him around 3:00 p.m. The maids apparently ended their day's work about 3:30 p.m. and traveled uptown to transfer or continue to Oaklawn. Although the signage requesting "colored patrons please be seated from rear" had been removed by then, almost invariably Black riders would begin seating in the rear of buses.

There were very few White riders that time of day and as we traversed the Selwyn area more and more maids boarded. Additional riders boarded at stops on McDowell Street which was in Brooklyn. When we arrived at the square, my father's bus was almost filled with Black people and the few

White people sitting within a few feet of each other. I wondered why the big deal over bus seating, nothing bad happened, just folks wanting to go from one place to another.

There was one incident of significance, and it was more than enlightening for me. It was summertime, my grandfather and I had been to the Carolina Theatre. We walked back to the square and waited for the State Street bus. It was about 3:30 p.m. as we stood against the side of Liggett Drugs where Bank of America Plaza is today. The bus arrived. State Street was not a heavy route and 32 passenger GMC coaches like 824, 825 were assigned. The 32 seat old looks had one forward facing twin seat just behind the rear door, and behind it a traverse seat over the rear wheels, then the full width rear seat. There were 8-10 riders on the bus. A Black man in a crumpled sport coat and hat boarded and sat on the traverse seat. He looked like he might have been from a janitorial staff of one of the buildings as he was not in laborers' clothing. The buses had a wide mirror of 12-16 inches for the driver to see the entire passenger compartment. I knew the driver.

Just before we pulled away from the square, I saw the driver's eyes in the mirror. They were burning into something; I knew they were eyes of anger. It could be only one thing; he was looking toward the Black man. We departed the square and then stopped at the next block in front of the Selwyn Hotel, a regular stop and a site now occupied by the Marriott City Center Hotel. He put the gear lever into neutral and sharply pulled up the handbrake on the left side of the driver's seat, stood up and marched back to the Black man. He yelled in loud, angry words to get on the rear seat. The Black man responded yes sir and quickly moved. The driver returned to his seat and the bus continued. Neither my grandfather nor I said anything until we got off the bus. We were shocked. It was 1955, I was ten. Perhaps the driver thought the man was testing limits, but that was hardly possible with so few riders and yet he was virtually at the back of the bus. I was learning fast.

There was something badly wrong here. I knew that White and Black people generally were separated in most circumstances. In my mind this was wrong. Nothing should cause this kind of treatment. It was anger and hate. The experience was the beginning of a divergence for me.

In the 1970s busing for school desegregation became a volatile political

Chapter 6 - Trains, Buses, and Cabs – But No Boats

issue. In the 1950s and 1960s we also had school buses, but with a difference. It was the result of transportation needs and not court mandated. I rode a city bus to Ashley Park Elementary in grades 5 and 6. Thousands of White children and Black children did so to many different schools. Duke Power offered reduced fare "school tickets" for children. Duke/City Coach also had designated school routes mornings and afternoons.

I was always assigned to schools closest to my place of residence. I enjoyed a ride with my friend Rusty Criminger to and from Wilmore Elementary in the first grade. Then Barringer (now Charles Parker Academic Center) opened and for the next two years I walked one mile each way, each day in all kinds of weather. I suspect my father might have been charged with child endangerment if it were 2025. We later moved to the other side of Wilkinson Blvd and the Ashley Park Elementary district. In the fifth and sixth grades we lived one mile from the school. I rode a city bus most days by walking four blocks to a nearby stop. I could also ride home or go uptown for dinner with my father but often I walked home in the afternoons.

With a few exceptions for peak hour routes for both Duke and City Coach routes were virtually unchanged in number and name for several decades. With suburban growth in the late fifties, City Coach geographically expanded several routes to better serve newer neighborhoods. I rode my father's bus, mostly on Saturdays between 1955 and 1960. Since we did not have an automobile between 1955 and 1959, I was not well-versed like the other guys on auto models and years. Determined to correct that inadequacy, during the fall of 1958 I learned autos through visual interpolation while riding my father's bus. I could then speak confidently about cars with the guys at school. By 1960, I was about to enter high school and there were too many things requiring my time. Riding with my father had come to an end.

City buses were still heavily utilized in the early 1960s but seemed less so to me. By then my bus travel was primarily to and from high school via a designated school route during my junior year. My girlfriend and I got on board at the corner of Berryhill Road and Morton Street and then the bus went to Herbert Spaugh Jr. High before arriving at Harry P. Harding High (new Harding and now Harding University High) on Alleghany Street. Often after I arrived home, I would take the No. 13 bus downtown as it passed by our duplex on Marlowe Avenue. I would buy my girlfriend a 45

RPM record or sometimes a charm for her bracelet. My other destinations were Belk, Morris and Barnes Grocery located at 227 West Trade next to the Hotel Charlotte (Carillon Building), or perhaps the Colonial Store at 209 North College (Truist Tower). Riding home with two bags of groceries was in no way embarrassing and quite convenient since the driver would let me off in front of our duplex.

After five years of riding buses, I had learned the city rather well; I had observed a lot of human interaction; I had a firsthand look at bankers, store clerks, maids, intellectuals and pretenders. Which one of the early sixties trips on No. 13 would be my last ride for decades? Neither. It turned out to be Memorial Day 1964. My friend David Atwood was in town, and I rode No. 2 to meet him and Jack Washam at the Square.

It was a great street education. Just ride, watch, and listen. It would be over twenty years before I set foot in another city bus. Since then, I have used express route buses only 3, maybe 4 times. I have taken my CPCC class uptown once by bus. The sensation is always eerily familiar and satisfying.

Intercity Buses

The junction of US 29, US 74 and US 21 made Charlotte a strategic location for intercity bus transportation. Greyhound and Trailways were the predominate providers for bus service. The Union Bus Terminal on West Trade Street (now The Kensington parking lot), only a couple of blocks from the Southern Railway Depot, was the epicenter of the action, but one might not know that by visual inspection alone.

The station was shoe-horned between two buildings where buses arriving entered an alley on the left side of the terminal, unloaded, and then parked in 45-degree slots on the right side with only a small driveway between buildings. The terminal had a requisite lunch counter and barber shop. I used the terminal only once. As it turned out, in 1977 a wheel bearing failure forced me to leave our 1971 LTD with an uncle in Wadesboro for repair. This necessitated my only use of the Union Bus Terminal.

In the early 2000s when the future of the site was uncertain, I was able to secure, intact, possession of the signature entrance feature of the terminal – an inset in the terra cotta tile entrance floor of a 1940 Flxible (correct spelling) bus, the model with an air scoop at the top rear of its roof. My intention was to present it to CATS for use in its future intermodal terminal. It was stored at a construction related business for a dozen or so years but somehow disappeared. The best laid plans of mice and men....

Trailways coaches were sub-lettered for regional entities – Continental Trailways, Smokey Mountain Trailways, and Queen City Trailways. Greyhound coaches were all part of Atlantic Greyhound. Trailways had a service facility on West Fifth Street only a few feet from the terminal. Decades later when the site became a parking lot there were environmental monitoring wells scattered over the property. No doubt a lot of contaminants had entered the soil over the decades. Greyhound had a much smaller office and single bay shop at 314 West Bland Street, just off South Mint. A few years later when City Coach built a new garage at 707 North Brevard both Trailways and Greyhound sent their coaches there for maintenance and servicing.

There were other bus systems that handled local markets. Sharon Coach Company serviced the Pineville area with possibly two separate routes, one via what is now the South Park area, the other following South Boulevard. Its buses would terminate at the Sharon Oil service station adjacent to the Builders Building, only a couple hundred feet from Union Bus Terminal. Both Mint Hill Bus Lines and Jackson Homes Bus Lines had city addresses at Union Terminal as late as 1959. However, I never saw coaches from either line.

When growing up it seemed everything was in greater variety than later decades. Buses were no exception. It was a game for me to see how many I could count on any given outing. While airlines and private automobiles inexorably became the primary means of transportation, it did not occur quickly. Intercity coaches and passenger trains were still heavily used throughout the 1950s. Beginning in the mid-1950s most new intercity buses were equipped with toilets and were air conditioned. During most of my childhood intercity buses were an entirely acceptable means of going places.

The *Charlotte Observer* noted on July 2, 1947, that Queen City Trailways had initiated "express" bus service to Asheville, and Wilmington, Carolina Beach and Myrtle Beach. Express service for buses, like with passenger trains, differed from "locals" which made all stops. The Wilmington service was serious competition with Seaboard's Rutherfordton – Wilmington passenger service which offered only one train a day.

In the 1940s (especially during the War years) a popular outing was a bus ride to Chimney Rock on a Sunday morning with a return home in the evening. How things have indeed changed. As it turns out, the so-called curbside coach service with on board power outlets and Wi-Fi service, especially on 100 - 250-mile routes, is again a popular service and is growing in some major metropolitan areas.

Taxis

For a city with so many buses, I saw a lot of taxi cabs and rode a few also. Being a transportation guy I was interested in cabs. I remember there were four cab providers. Yellow Cab was the big one – Edison 2-4141. Even a child could recognize their cabs were cleaner, or perhaps it was their shiny yellow paint. Yellow Cab was located at 317 South Poplar. The others were Victory Cab (black and white) with headquarters in an old service station on the southeast corner of Brevard and East Fourth Streets. Red Top (black and red) was located four blocks north on Brevard Street. Baker Cab (black and green) was dispatched from 631 North Tryon. Yellow Cab enjoyed the longevity the other three did not have. Cabs were a necessity for many without automobiles, and there were a lot of people without vehicles in the fifties. Cabs could be useful for those such as ladies who worked late shifts at Bell Telephone located at 200 North Caldwell. Cabs were regular transportation for other occupations, the hours of which did not coincide with bus service.

I rode cabs to and from my grandmother's house on State Street. I did so in rainy and cold weather. In good weather I could walk the one-mile trek in 15 minutes, and much of the route had no sidewalks. I knew it was a mile because the cab fare meter would still register the base $0.45 when we entered her driveway. With a dime tip the total was $0.55. I discovered just how precise the distance traveled was in an odd way. In the 1950s Yellow Cabs were always Plymouths. Occasionally a Dodge would be in the mix. They were basic models with straight drive transmissions, no amenities except heaters – yes, a heater was optional on most of the low price three automobile models. The 1956 Plymouths used 15-inch wheels. Like both

Chapter 6 - Trains, Buses, and Cabs – But No Boats

Ford and Chevrolet, Plymouth changed to 14-inch wheels in 1957 in keeping with the low profile, fin bedecked styling of the time.

Somehow an anomaly with the wheel sizes caused the fare meters to trip to $0.55 when the cab would cross over the sidewalk into the driveway. My grandmother's house was the first one on the left after turning onto State Street from Tuckasegee Road. The necessity of holding on to that additional dime yielded a creative solution. I would tell the driver to just pull over to the side of the street – no curb and gutter there then. The few feet less in distance of travel prevented the meter from tripping and the dime was mine. On a few occasions I rode a cab to school if it were raining heavily.

On October 1, 1958, City Coach drivers, who were members of the Brotherhood of Railway Trainmen Union, went on strike. The walkout lasted for twenty-five days. My father found temporary employment with Victory Cab. He drove a six-cylinder powered 1955 Chevrolet 210 sedan which he kept at our duplex during the night hours. It was not our vehicle, but it was nice to have a car in the driveway and have a few rides to the nearby grocery store.

Chapter Notes

Pinoca: Name given to an unincorporated community on the general area of Rozzells Ferry Road between Hovis Road and Hoskins Road. Pinoca supposedly stood for Piedmont and Northern Company. P&N's main freight yard and engine service facilities were located at Pinoca, and freight cars could be interchanged there with Seaboard which ran parallel to P&N at that location.

Swift Distribution Plant at 400 South Mint Street. It was served by the Piedmont and Northern Railway from a P&N spur track that ran down the center of Mint Street.

Duke Power Bus Systems: Duke Power provided electrically powered street cars for nine North and South Carolina cities. The initial contracts were based on Duke being the only electric utility and its ability to construct and maintain the necessary overhead catenary wires to power streetcars. When streetcar systems were terminated in favor of transit buses those contracts were continued with Duke being the sole provider. The last Duke served city was Greensboro and that service was sold to a private provider in 1991.

This photo is purported to be the last passenger train to stop at the West Trade Southern depot. In the background and just to the left of the power pole the depot tower can be faintly seen. The roofs covering the platforms are discernable. The former coach yard on the left was being used for freight car storage. The track on the right is only two blocks away from the main US Post Office and is populated with head end cars – baggage, express, and mail. The US Government cancelled all rail mail contracts in 1967. Mail had been the profit component that kept passenger service in play. A consequent was prompt termination of countless passenger trains and that was the predicate for the creation of Amtrak that began service on May 1, 1971. Southern Railway did not join Amtrak until 1979 and continued to run its few passenger trains with considerable pride under Southern President W. Graham Claytor who, after his retirement, served 11 years as head of Amtrak. The two lead locomotives are Alco RS-3 freight road switchers. They do not have stream generators for passenger coach heating and are almost certainly being "deadheaded" to Atlanta for heavy maintenance. This train might be Southern's southbound Washington – Atlanta "Piedmont". Photo: Robinson Spangler Carolina Room, Public Library of Charlotte- Mecklenburg County.

Seaboard Depot. Photos of the Seaboard passenger station are scarce since the depot was and still is virtually hidden at the end of North College Street, above North Tryon Street. In the fifties Charlotte was served by only two Seaboard daily trains: Train 13 from Wilmington arrived at 10:40 PM, and Train 14 to Wilmington departed at 4:20 AM – not optimum times for photographs. Each offered connections with the New York-Miami Palmland at Seaboard's Hamlet NC hub. The final Seaboard passenger service ended in late 1958. The building, listed on the National Register of Historic Places, was used by the Seaboard and its successor roads for some years. It is now owned and used by The Center for Urban Ministries. This photo was likely taken in the 1970s as the first pickup truck is a 1969 Chevrolet and there are two 1973 or later Chevrolets farther down the line of vehicles. The building was designed by noted Charlotte architect C. C. Hook. Photo: Robinson Spangler Carolina Room, Public Library of Charlotte-Mecklenburg County.

Now Arriving from Charlotte. Photos of Seaboard activity in Charlotte are almost non-existent. Here is Seaboard Train No 14 from Charlotte about two blocks from the historic Hamlet Depot at 8:15 a.m. on March 25, 1950. The consist (railroad term) is a baggage/express car, an RPO (railway post office car – for picking up mail on "the fly" and sorting in route), and a single coach. Its 4:20 AM departure probably had something to do with its light patronage. No. 14 would take most of that day to reach Wilmington. Passengers could connect to New York-Florida trains at Hamlet's historic 1900 vintage station that is still in use for north-south Amtrak trains. Photo: Used with permission of Withers Publishing; Paul K. Withers/David W. Salter Seaboard Motive Power, Withers Publishing 1988.

Norfolk Southern – North Brevard Street. Elusive though it was in my childhood, I finally was able to take this 1972 photo showing a Norfolk Southern (pre-1974) freight with four GP-18 locos heading out of Charlotte with Train 64 bound for Raliegh and Norfolk. The location is North Brevard Street in the present area of Festivus Court. CATS North Brevard Light Rail Facility and its line north have completely changed the landscape in this area and NS successor Aberdeen, Carolina, and Western's entry was relocated to the west closer to the present Norfolk Southern yard. Photo: Author's collection.

Norfolk Southern - Brevard Street Terminus. This late fifty's view looking north was likely taken from north of 16th Street at the Norfolk Southern (original) yard office. Brevard Street is on the right. The Southern Railway main yard is on the left. Photo: Courtesy Dalton McDonald.

North Brevard - 2025. Looking north to NoDa. This is the previous view from a higher angle to depict new residential construction. A CATS North Brevard Light Rail Facility is in the center of the photo. The former Southern Railway Yard, now Norfolk Southern, remains on the left. Photo: Google Earth.

Wesley Heights – Summit Avenue. Probably an early 1940s scene of a two-unit P& N interurban run from Charlotte to Gastonia. The lead car is about to cross Summit Avenue. Interurban equipment differed from street cars as it was railroad compatible, i.e. running gear, couplers, etc. and capable of much higher speeds. It was an earlier iteration of the Rail Diesel Cars that were widely used somewhat later but without an overhead electrical catenary. Although a hazy day one can see why Wesley Heights, developed in the 1920s, was so named – its three primary streets offered a view of downtown. Photo: Used with Permission of Golden West Books, Piedmont and Northern, The Great Electric System of the South, 1974.

Summit Avenue Today. With new construction and many rehabs, Wesley Heights is quite desirable one hundred years later. It is a good representation of a close to center city neighborhood in resurgence. The P & N right-of-way is now a trail, and rails are still in place here. A decades old crossing gate control cabinet is still extant behind the camera that captured this photo. Google photo.

> APPEAL OF MERRY OAKS CIVIC CLUB FOR BUS SERVICE TO MEET EMERGENCY NEED.
>
> Representatives of the Merry Oaks Civic Club appeared before Council with regard to bus service in the Central Avenue Extension and Chantilly areas. Mrs. L. B. Andrews stressed the urgency of the need for bus service in the eastern area of the city, which she stated is and has been a state of emergency since the extension of the city limits in 1949 to include this area. She discussed at length the efforts of the Club to secure bus service for the area, the hardships realized by citizens of the area in getting to and from work because of the lack of busses, the inability of their children to reach schools, the dangers to the children using bicycles on congested highways enroute to schools due to no busses being available, the attitude of the City Officials in not cooperating with the citizens in their efforts to secure needed busses and the inefficiency of Duke Power Company in not providing needed service. She stated the citizens of the area are entitled to being adequately served by the City's public transportation system and that they demand such service.

Demand for Bus Service. For a time after WWII bus service was almost an essential need for many neighborhoods. The passage above is a part of Charlotte City Council proceedings, October 4, 1950; Minute Book 33, Page 386. Duke Power had attempted a shuttle service route, but it was discontinued after a short time. Residents demanded bus service. Image: Charlotte City Council Minute Book 33, Page 386.

My father was at the helm of 1002, end of the No 7, Biddleville Line sometime in early 1956. 1002 was a GM TDH-5105. These were the largest buses in Charlotte for many years. Forty feet long and 102 inches wide (legal limit) instead of the usual 96 inches. Route Nos 7 and 16 were the most used routes and received the largest buses.

The farebox was locked and all were removed each evening when buses returned to the garage. Beyond the farebox was a metal bracket that was secured to the steering column on which he had placed his changer needed for riders who had only bills. There were no bank cards scanners or monthly passes then. Photo: Author's collection.

Route Map. This is a City Coach route system map from September 1959. Peak hour route extensions are shown in broken lines and are largely on the east and south sides of the city reflecting growth which had already begun away from the west side. For a time, bus routes did a credible job of servicing newer residential areas. Express routes were still two decades away. The No 9 State Street route of 1957 had been dropped, reflecting a ridership change in that neighborhood area. Photo: Aurthor's collection.

City Coach Bus Garage. East 11th Street at North Brevard. This 1973 photo depicts the bus garage and lot, just visible over the roofs of the coaches, as it remained for several decades. The garage itself opened in 1957, replacing the former Duke Power trolley garage on South Blvd. Soon it served both Greyhound and Trailways coaches. Only the 32 story Jefferson First Union Building, the bus advertising placards, and the signage atop the former Hotel Barringer offer any clue that it was not 1960. GM "old look" 1035 reposes at the end of a line of GM "new look" coaches that begin filling the bus ranks in 1959. The old looks, a superb industrial design, were built between 1940 and 1959, although some smaller coaches were continued until 1968. Production totaled about 38,000 units. Most City Coach units ran out their remaining days rather ignominiously as school buses adorned with stop signs and ugly red lights on the rear end of their roofs. Also shown is a Duke Power School Ticket from the 1950s. Photo: Author's collection.

4 PARK ROAD or AVONDALE

From Square to Park Road or Avondale	From Park Road or Avondale to Square

MONDAY THRU FRIDAY

A. M.	A. M.
5.49,.56*.	5.42*,.56,.57*,
6.04,.12*,.19,.27*,.34,.42*,.49,.56*	6.11,.11*,.26,.27*,.41,.42*,.56,.57*
7.04,.12*,.19,.27*,.34,.42*,.49,.56*,	7.11,.11*,.26,.27*,.41,.42*,.56,.57*
8.04,.12*,.19,.27*,.34,.42*,.49	8.11,.11*,.26,.27*,.41,.42*,.56,.57*
9.04,.15,.30,.45	9.07,.22,.37,.52
10.00,.15,.30,.45	10.07,.22,.37,.52
11.00,.15,.30,.45	11.07,.22,.37,.52

P. M.	P. M.
12.00,.15,.30,.45	12.07,.22,.37,.52
1.00,.15,.30,.45	1.07,.22,.37,.52
2.00,.15,.30,.45,.56*	2.07,.22,.37,.56,.57*
3.00,.12*,.15,.27*,.34,.42*,.49,.56*	3.11,.11*,.26,.27*,.41,.42*,.56,.57*
4.04,.12*,.19,.27*,.34,.42*,.49,.56*	4.11,.11*,.26,.27*,.41,.42*,.56,.57*
5.04,.12*,.19,.27*,.34,.42*,.49,.56*	5.11,.11*,.26,.27*,.41,.42*,.56,.57*
6.04,.20,.40	6.11,.20,.40
7.00,.20,.40	7.00,.20,.40
8.00,.20,.40	8.00,.20,.40
9.00,.20,.40	9.00,.20,.40
10.00,.20,.40	10.00,.20,.40
11.00,.20,.30	11.00,.20
* Avondale only	* From Avondale

SATURDAY ONLY

A. M.	A. M.
6.15,.30,.45	5.52
7.00,.15,.30,.45	6.07,.22,.37,.52
8.00,.15,.27*,.30,.42*,.49,.56*	7.07,.22,.37,.52,.57*
9.04,.12*,.19,.27*,.34,.42*,.49,.56*	8.07,.11*,.26,.27*,.41,.42*,.56,.57*
10.04,.12*,.19,.27*,.34,.42*,.49,.56*	9.11,.11*,.26,.27*,.41,.42*,.56,.57*
11.04,.12*,.19,.27*,.34,.42*,.49,.56*	10.11,.11*,.26,.27*,.41,.42*,.56,.57*
	11.11,.11*,.26,.27*,.41,.42*,.56,.57*

P. M.	P. M.
12.04,.12*,.19,.27*,.34,.42*,.49,.56*	12.11,.11*,.26,.27*,.41,.42*,.56,.57*
1.04,.12*,.19,.27*,.34,.42*,.49,.56*	1.11,.11*,.26,.27*,.41,.42*,.56,.57*
2.04,.12*,.19,.27*,.34,.42*,.49,.56*	2.11,.11*,.26,.27*,.41,.42*,.56,.57*
3.04,.12*,.19,.27*,.34,.42*,.49,.56*	3.11,.11*,.26,.27*,.41,.42*,.56,.57*
4.04,.12*,.19,.27*,.34,.42*,.49,.56*	4.11,.11*,.26,.27*,.41,.42*,.56,.57*
5.04,.12*,.19,.27*,.34,.42*,.49,.56*	5.11,.11*,.26,.27*,.41,.42*,.56,.57*
6.04,.20,.40	6.11,.20,.40
7.00,.20,.40	7.00,.20,.40
8.00,.20,.40	8.00,.20,.40
9.00,.20,.40	9.00,.20,.40
10.00,.20,.40	10.00,.20,.40
11.00,.20,.30	11.00,.20
* Avondale only	* From Avondale

SUNDAY ONLY

A. M.	A. M.
7.00,.20,.40	7.00,.20,.40
8.00,.20,.40	8.00,.20,.40
9.00,.20,.40	9.00,.20,.40
10.00,.20,.40	10.00,.20,.40
11.00,.20,.40	11.00,.20,.40

Duke Power Schedule. This is the No. 4 Route schedule from October 1952. Route No. 4 was titled Belmont – Parkwood and Park Road – Avondale. The base route served the heavy residential area surrounding Park Road and the former mill area in the Belmont neighborhood. The Parkwood and Avondale subtitles derived were streets served during "peak ours". It conveys a lot about lifestyles in 1952. Eight departures an hour during weekday morning and afternoon peaks are indicative of the demand for service. Noteworthy is the Saturday schedule, which illustrates the volume of shoppers who visited downtown throughout the day. Automobiles proliferated after WWII but 1952 was during the Korean War and the post Korean War explosion of economic growth, of which automobiles were a large component, had not fully matured. Park Road Shopping Center had not opened yet so primary shopping still took place downtown. Photo: Author's Collection.

The First Diesel Buses. This Duke Archives photo was dated 3-13-50. These are the first twelve diesel buses that Duke purchased, GM TDH-3612 models, numbers 844 through 855. Although not discernable in this print, the destination boards for each coach had one of the Duke Routes posted in descending order. Today's drivers can simply key in the destination and number for a digital LED display. Duke drivers for years had to turn a hand crank to retrieve the correct route destination, then change it at the end of the line with each cycle so it would read correctly for the opposite direction of the route. The building in the background is a Duke coal gasification plant that was probably inactive when the photo was taken. There were two large storage tanks just outside the left of the photo. Photo: Courtesy Duke Energy Company.

Silversides or "New Look". This is a 1972 GM T6H-4523. It is a 35-foot coach formerly of Charlotte Transit and now owned by the Charlotte-Mecklenburg Historic Landmarks Commission. It has been restored to a nearly new condition. The first of the new look coaches arrived in late 1959 and in 1960 the first air-conditioned coaches were in service. The angled side windows reflected the design of GM intercity buses. The 'silversides" moniker derived from the natural finish stainless steel fluted side panels which were painted once Charlotte assumed ownership of the system in 1976. Photo: Aurthor's collection.

Union Bus Station. 416-424 West Trade Street. The 1941 building, a simpler derivation of Art Deco, was little changed in this early 2000s photo. Like any large city station, it had a barber shop, a restaurant, Travelers' Aid Society, and lots of pay phones. The following photo depicts the site in 2020. Coaches entered the alley way on the left, unloaded, then pulled under the canopy visible in the background of the right side. It did not lend itself to repurposing and was demolished. Photo: Author's collection.

Former Union Bus Staton. Same view today and one of three structures between the former departure drive and North Pine Street seen on right. Google photo.

May 29, 1951 (recessed from May 28, 1951)
Minute Book 34 -Page 35

RECESSED MEETING RECONVENED AT 4:30 O'CLOCK P.M. ON TUESDAY, MAY 29, 1951.

The recessed meeting on May 28, 1951 was reconvened at 4:30 o'clock p.m., on Tuesday, May 29th, with Mayor Shaw presiding, and Councilmen Albea, Baxter, Boyd, Coddington, Dellinger, Jordan and Van Every present.

INVOCATION.

The invocation was given by Councilman Claude L. Albea.

DISCUSSION OF PLAN FOR OPERATION OF TAXICABS DURING BUS DRIVERS STRIKE.

Mayor Shaw stated that because of the critical situation due to the bus drivers strike, the representatives of the taxicab companies were requested to be present at the informal conference of the Council prior to this meeting, and at this meeting, to discuss the taxicab operation during the emergency and to assist in the formulation of a policy under which they could operate without working a hardship on either the Cab Companies or the cab riders. Representatives of Taxicab Companies present were Mr. R. E. Crump and Mr. Brock Barkley, Attorney, for the Yellow Cab Company, Mr. Keith Beaty for Red Top Cab Company, Mr. R. A. Isenhour for Victory Cab Company and Mr. E. R. Baker for Baker Cab Company.

Two ordinances which were drawn by Mr. John D. Shaw, City Attorney, after conferences this morning with representatives of the four cab companies, were considered by the Council and discussed.

In the discussion Mr. Barkley, Attorney for Yellow Cab Company, stated in their opinion the citizens do not expect the City to request the Cab Companies to assume a financial loss because of the bus strike. That a call service is as essential as the demand for cruising or pick-up service. That cabs cannot cruise over any appreciable area of the city and call service must be depended upon. That call service is essential to those persons going to and from hospitals, doctors' offices and to travelers by bus, rail and air and for employees of industrial establishments who have contracts for such service. That the maintenance of a call service makes necessary the use of meters and the continuance of the meter fares. That they believe the present rate is reasonable and actually lower than the 25¢ per head rate on the cruising service. That Yellow Cab Company has no objection whatsoever to any service the Council wishes to adopt so long as it does not affect the present meter system and meter rates under which they operate and wish to continue to do so. He stated further that since the strike Yellow Cab Company has carried twice as many passengers but the revenue increase has been a little less than 25 percent. That at least one-third of their trips before the strike were 35 cent fares, and 60 percent of their runs are less than 55 cents, and their

Buses and Cabs. Critical Infrastructure. This document is the first page from the Charlotte City Council meeting of May 21, 1951. This was essentially an emergency management action by the Council to ensure taxicab resources to all citizens during the first strike ever of Duke Power bus drivers. This depicts that both buses and taxi cabs were critical components of the city's transportation infrastructure in 1951. Image: Charlotte City Council Meeting Book 34, Page 35.

Chapter 7
Schools, Churches, and Other Places

The *Leave It to Beaver* television show of 1957 – 1963 accurately portrayed much of contemporary 1950/1960s life. School, whether elementary, junior or senior high, was the fulcrum of a kid's existence, at least in my world. The parental doctrine of that time was: be at school, behave as expected, have no arguments with teachers, and learn so we could have more prosperous lives and be good contributing citizens. In twelve years of education, I did not hear a four-letter word inside a classroom. Gambling was not permitted, and students were known to have been "sent to the office" for matching pennies.

Charlotte City and Mecklenburg County ran separate systems for most of the time I was in public education. "Colored" or Black schools were segregated within those systems. In 1953 there were five high schools within the city: Second Ward and West Charlotte (Black), and Central, Harding, and Myers Park (White). I simply accepted schools were separated by race and did not fully understand the rationale other than there were intense feelings about race among many White people. In fact, like my peers, I did not challenge anything. Not then. I did not yet have bona fides to engage adults on matters of societal norms. The first integration of Charlotte City Schools took place in the fall of 1957. There were no Black students in any of the schools I attended through graduation.

School architecture changed dramatically in the 1950s. School buildings of the prewar years were usually two-story edifices that conveyed institutional solidarity. A gym or cafeteria might be an appendage, but the administration and classrooms were contained withing the primary structure. For instance, Central High of 1923 looked like a citadel on Elizabeth Avenue. The structure survives and is the "Central Building" for Central Piedmont Community College. UNC-Charlotte began in its basement classrooms in 1949 and was known as Charlotte College.

Many new schools had wings of multiple classrooms in some orderly arrangement and connected by covered sidewalks to administrative and cafeteria spaces. Ashely Park had its restrooms in a separate structure outside the classroom wings as there was apparently less concern for security at the time. The classrooms had hopper windows on each side which helped ventilate spaces in hot weather. The concrete slab floors at Ashley Park were heated by electrical resistance units and the classrooms were quite comfortable in winter. The design offered a lot of open views and easy access to the outside and playgrounds, but it was a bone-chilling experience when going to the lunchroom on a cold, rainy, and windy day.

I attended first grade at Wilmore Elementary, circa 1922, at the corner of West Boulevard and South Mint Street. An imposing two-story building with steam radiators, with high ceilings, and transoms over classroom doors to better ventilate the rooms. The architecture conveyed a sense of fortress-like security to this first grader. Once inside I felt safe and secure. I rode to and from school with a neighbor that first year. Wilmore later became a staff development center. At this writing the building may possibly be designated for repurposing by a private preservation organization.

Noteworthy was the nearby A. G. Junior High of similar design that opened in 1923, pioneering the junior high concept in North Carolina of grouping grades 7 through 9. A.G. closed at the end of the 1957-1958 school year to be replaced by a new school of the same name at 1800 Runnymede Lane. The Dowd YMCA has occupied the former A. G. site at 400 East Morehead Street since. As it turned out, Barringer School (now Charles Parker Academy) on Walton Avenue opened in 1952 and I was assigned there. Once we moved to the north side of Wilkinson Boulevard, I became a student at another fifties "modern design" elementary – Ashley Park. Both schools have since been completely rebuilt with a different design concept. At Ashley Park Mrs. Jeanne Sullivan read from a book titled "Call It Courage" once a week What a welcome break it was. Shooting marbles before school began was an immensely satisfying game of skill. However, shooting Marbles was a fad and had a very short half-life.

Every morning (in home rooms for our junior and senior high years) we had a devotion, a prayer, and a pledge to the flag. Students usually took turns leading this part of home room activity. Any student not of the Christian faith simply sat quietly during the devotion and prayer. Most of my friends were protestants. A few were Catholics. Only one I recall was Jewish.

Chapter 7 - Schools, Churches, and Other Places

Only a relatively few nations have a pledge to their flag and ours was adopted by Congress in 1942, the first full year of WWII. Apparently, it was during WWII that the Pledge became a regular part of one's school day. While school systems were prohibited by court decisions from requiring students to recite it, all of us dutifully did so. The pledge day after day seemed somehow to diminish real patriotism I thought. In hindsight a citizen pledge to exercise good citizenship would have been a much better alternative. The prayer and devotional reading on the other hand, while it clearly injected religion into education, provided a few minutes of quiet focus and worshipful personal introspection that was not wasted at the beginning of one's day. Did it make us a better generation? As my friend Jim Carter said: we were a well-behaved and respectful generation because there was a better than even chance if someone saw us doing otherwise our parents might learn about it.

It was the era of Elvis. No boy I can recall wore headgear in the winter. On cold winter days the water we copiously used to style our long hair, along with Vaseline Hair Oil, Wild Root Cream Oil, or a similarly viscous hair tonic, would freeze so that our hair would become stiff with ice. Upon arrival at the field in front of Ashley Park we would check our hair and on cold mornings we would have hair filled with ice crystals. In the seventh grade, many guys would drop in the boy's room between each class period, wet our hair over the sinks, comb it again, and then on to our next classes.

The confluence of several things started the demise of the wet head. In the mid to late 1950s hair spray in propellent cans became readily available in the marketplace. A decades old hair dressing, Brylcream, began a new ad campaign about the time a new TV program 77 Sunset Strip hit the airwaves. A regular on the program, Ed "Kookie" Byrnes, regularly combed his heavy dome of perfect hair. Byrnes had a dry look without any heavy petroleum products to keep hair plastered in place. That was it for me. I became a Revlon hair spray guy, as did thousands of others, acknowledging it or not.

An especially vivid memory is of an afternoon in the sixth grade. For the second consecutive year, someone from downtown – the school system administrative offices – whose name was Mrs. Hays would visit our combined classes for a special session on sex education.

Our teacher had segregated boys and girls within the room, and we were given instructions that laughing or talking would not be tolerated. Under the windows adjacent to the exterior wall were bookcases with magazines. One of Mrs. Hays' first actions was to draw a certain human organ on the board at the precise time that my lifelong friend Craig Pergerson held up a cartoon in *North Carolina Wildlife* magazine.

Our group of boys burst out laughing. To say the teacher was flushed red would be charitable, her eyes were beaming energy, and I was in her sight. It was a long afternoon for some of us. In retrospect it is astonishing that in the very religious and conservative south, a small southern city would be so enlightened and progressive. It was a fortuitously good thing. Conversations with classmates decades later validated the enlightened judgement of our educators. None of my classmates received any sex education from their parents!

When it opened in 1957 on Camp Green Street (1901 Herbert Spaugh Lane), I entered seventh grade at Herbert Spaugh Junior High, named for school board member and Pastor of Little Church on the Lane, Bishop Herbert S. Spaugh. It had the same familiar low-profile design but congregated its classrooms in two wings. There was no air conditioning except in the offices. In grade 7 we had a diverse syllabus including one quarter of home economics, one of music, one of physical education and one of industrial arts. To build our social skills, when our alternating schedules had gym class on a Friday, we would have dancing class. Into the gym we went, took off our shoes, all the boys lined up on one side, girls on the other, and on command the boys rushed to the other side to pair with a girl. The girls were never allowed to run to the boys.

For a while our school had a juke box available during lunch hours in the courtyard area near the gym. The distant resonance of Dee Clark or Lloyd Price would often uplift my spirits before lunch time. Not surprisingly ours was an era of clothing fads. I never had a Madras shirt and felt stylish only once during that time. Deck pants for young men hit the scene in the spring of 1959 and lasted only through the summer. They were like girl's pedal pushers but with a short slit at the bottom of each side seam of which had two-stripe contrasting colors. The legs stopped short of the wearer's socks. I had two pairs, a black one and a white one, each came with a rope belt of soft cotton. They were so ephemeral that no one dared to wear them at the start of the next school year, less than three months away.

It was at Spaugh when we experienced three significant winter storms on three consecutive Wednesdays in March of 1960. A cumulative total of 19.5 inches fell on March 2, 9, and 16. I always walked to and from Spaugh. The fact is we all walked a lot to get around. My pal Bill Jenkins sometimes walked his girlfriend home from Spaugh to her home in Smallwood. Love does conquer all. Spaugh closed in June 2011 and is now a CMS administrative center.

It was late August 1960, and it was time to enter the adult world. Harding High School awaited. Securely ensconced within the tall trees at the end of Irwin Avenue was the school known throughout the state for its athletic prowess. Between 1952 and 1954 Harding held the nation consecutive win record for football, 35 – 0. It was a 1935 design anchored on one end by its columnated gym and on the other by a similarly adorned auditorium. It conveyed the ambience of a quiet university. I had heard about its tough instructors, about bullies, good and bad things, you name it. Many of Harding's original faculty from 1935 remained until they retired in the late 1960s. Newer arrivals had the same professional ethic as the original instructors. They were a family. They were dedicated to our young people, period. A few of them may at times have seemed off center to us, but all worked together dedicated to their task. Many students, myself included, had parents who had been instructed by these good folks.

We all had heard about Flora Mae Watson, instructor of plane geometry. While she truly seemed old, I am now much older than she was then. Her room was on the east end of the second floor near the top of the stairs. As Stan Morgan correctly recalls, on the first day of class she took a piece of notebook paper and crumpled it and left it on the floor near the door. No one picked it up upon entering the room. She then told us of her disappointment that none of us had pride in our school! We were required to make book covers for our textbooks. I suspect her overbearing presence may have impacted some students for their lifetimes. Almost everyone in her classes learned geometry. I did it out of cold fear. I always could do my proof when I was called to the board. Her room was a stressful place. Mr. James Hawkins, principal for over three decades, once told our class reunion he could tell who the best teachers were because the students always remember the tough ones. Perhaps. It was good to leave that classroom behind.

My mother was in Harding's first graduating class; it was unspoken I must do well. It was the best year of my high school career. Harding closed at the end of the 1960-1961 year, but the facility remained open but not as a high school. It was rebuilt in the 1990s as Irwin Academy (elementary plus kindergarten) with its signature gym and auditorium facades still anchoring at either end. "New" Harding opened at 1901 Alleghany Street in fall of 1961. It was the "George Jetson" era of design, but Harding's design character was muted and looked somewhat attractive relative to its time. It grouped functional buildings around a quadrangle. In a novel approach to dining, it had three remote dining areas served by a central kitchen. It is now Harding University High and even with newer buildings much of its 1961 architectural character manifests itself.

Two events worth noting. In the fall of 1961, virtually every boy wore white crew socks. It had been the standard for decades. Someone, his name long forgotten, wore a pair of the new Gold Cup brand of orlon/nylon socks that came in various colors. Several other upper-class guys followed within a couple of days. I thought the look was so cool I had to have a couple of pairs. Belk, downtown of course, was open on Monday and Friday evenings. The next Monday my father drove me downtown; I got out and went into the store while he circled the block a couple of times. Gold Cups were $1.50 a pair, pricey for 1961. Belk's Archdale brand was only $0.79, so I purchased several pairs and joined Harding's fashion elite. Within two weeks white crew socks had all but disappeared from campus.

The other happening appears to have been a "covert" operation between the school superintendent and the publisher of the two Charlotte daily newspapers, the *Charlotte Observer* and the *Charlotte News*. When my senior year began in the closing days of August 1962 there was a new student on campus, a senior. He looked a little older and we were told a son of a military man who had lived around the globe, and he needed a few courses to fulfill his diploma requirements. He was, in fact, a recent UNC Chapel Hill graduate who worked for the *News* and had been planted, embedded being a better description, in the Harding student body.

The idea was he would get to know the students, instructors, and school spirit at our newest high school and write thereof. Frank Timson was a

Chapter 7 - Schools, Churches, and Other Places

recent NC State graduate and in his first teaching position when, on his first morning at school, he was called into the office and told the full story about this new kid in his homeroom class. The cover worked for two weeks and then was followed by three days of front-page coverage. The reporter was young Alex Coffin of The *Charlotte News* (which ceased publication in 1985).

Following my junior year, it was time to validate myself as a young adult and that meant finding employment. Newspaper delivery was not for me. The A & P at 2400 Freedom Drive was within walking distance. The hours were good, and the pay was $1.00 per hour. I began my working career in July 1962. I bagged groceries and did stock work. I was responsible for the paper aisle and on Saturdays I put out all the frozen foods that had been delivered during the night. Saturdays usually had Morton Cream Pies at three for a dollar. That kept me off the bagging lines until late in the day. I always bagged for Mr. Way who would bring his 1960 Pontiac Parisienne to the curb in front of the store. He liked his groceries placed in the trunk and there were always two quarters lying on the floor of the trunk as tipping was not allowed. A paltry amount perhaps, but it purchased two gallons of gasoline at the off-brand gas station at the front of the store parking lot.

May 27, 1963, David Ovens Auditorium, 7:00 p.m. Graduation time. Harding had fewer students than in the years at the original school - 180 diplomas were bestowed. The next morning, I realized what had just happened. I did not really know what to do with myself. I was happy, but school had always been an important place for me. I had to engage the changes at hand. I enrolled in Charlotte College for the fall semester. I wanted to be an engineer. I paid $300 to enroll, books not included. I was not fully prepared for independence, which required personal discipline. Interestingly, in later years friends and colleagues would tell me I have more discipline than anyone they knew. A little of it would have been of significant help in 1963.

A week after graduation my father traded our 1954 Ford for a 1961 Ford Galaxie Club Victoria. It was black and I kept it spotless. I would often back up into a slot on the second row of Barbeque King on Wilkinson Boulevard, enjoy onion rings with a friend or two, and watch my friends and classmates cruise through the "King", all while we listened songs like Blue Velvet, Hey

There Loney Boy, It's My Party, Easier Said Than Done, and Candy Girl sometimes with an early moon setting in the west. It was a great summer.

The "King" is still there, unchanged, but likely on borrowed time since the Wilkinson corridor and surrounding neighborhoods are in demand and property value underneath the "King" is no doubt soaring.

Our graduating class held its first reunion event in 1973. Then in 1983 we began holding reunions every five years without interruption. This in addition to quarterly luncheons for the past dozen years or so, supplemented with parties celebrating strategic birthdays. A quarterly newsletter has kept us connected. I regularly speak with five of my classmates, one from across the Atlantic, via Zoom. It is like nothing has changed. They are all still eighth graders at Spaugh in my memory.

Church

Not everyone attended church, but it seemed like most of us did. Churches were so numerous they required four full columns in the city directory of 1957. On Sunday evenings church bells were a common sound. The so called "first" churches were in place as were the three big Myers Park churches. Covenant Presbyterian was new at Morehead and Dilworth with Temple Israel across Dilworth Road from it. St Peters Catholic Church at 507 South Tryon dated to the 1890s. East Boulevard had Dilworth Methodist and Holy Trinity Greek Orthodox churches on its streetside. House of Prayer for All People was located on South McDowell.

My mother's family were members at Wesley Heights Methodist, corner of Grandin Road and West 4th Street in the heart of Wesley Heights, a 1920s neighborhood. She was the organist there until her death. I attended Sunday school with kids with whom I later graduated. For the 11:00 service, I sat with my grandparents on a pew aligned with a memorial plaque set into the stained-glass window framing. It honored my mother. My father always worked on Sundays as there were drivers who wanted a day off and he was forever on the job. I sat relatively still and quiet as my grandmother expected that of me. Putting on "Sunday clothes" transferred an expectation that the wearer was to comport in a manner in keeping with the surroundings and societal norms. Thanks to my grandmother's discipline, I can still be motionless and quiet without difficulty.

Chapter 7 - Schools, Churches, and Other Places

We did not attend Sunday evening services. I do remember hearing chimes from a nearby church at about 5:45 p.m. each Sunday afternoon. I suspect Television was responsible for decline of evening services. Baptist churches had Wednesday evening Prayer Meetings. During my junior high years, I attended a neighborhood church with school friends – Greenland Avenue Baptist on the corner of Berryhill Road and Greenland. Everyone knew Baptists had the best meals so dinner before prayer meetings on Wednesday was a big incentive to be present. That lasted about a year.

My grandmother (Annie) was a Sunday School teacher. She lived her faith but did not push it on others. She never combined her religion with politics. About every two or three weeks we would visit the mausoleum at Forest Lawn West after Sunday lunch. My mother's crypt was near the south side building entrance where it would receive afternoon sunlight. My grandmother would carefully arrange fresh flowers in the workroom and then leave them in a clean vase on the granite mullion below the crypt. Adjacent to the stairs that led to the upper level there was a door. I never saw it open and for a while when I was about six I thought God lived behind it.

Then as now, many churches had summer "Bible Schools" for children, usually lasting about two weeks. All the scout packs and troops were sponsored by churches. There were also various activities and occasional trips and summer camps to occupy young people during their idle summer hours. I was not a scout until at fifteen I became an Explorer Scout. Many of my friends were scouts and always their packs or troops were church sponsored. While church was a big part of our lives, there seemed to be an understanding that religion and government could co-exist.

North Carolina prohibited certain commercial/business enterprises from being open to the public on Sundays. The only businesses open on Sundays were some drug stores, some gas stations, and restaurants. Buses used Sunday/holiday schedules. A block away from my grandmother's home was Blair Drugs at the corner of Tuckasegee Road and Alice Avenue. Like many drug stores around the city, they had milk, bread, ice cream and a few other essentials. Other grocery items were out of reach as Sunday "blue laws" prohibited supermarkets from being open. Movie theaters could open after church hours but had to close at 6:00 p.m. They then could reopen at 8:30 p.m. in the evening, after church hours. That began to change in the early 1960s led in part by some court challenges and perhaps a reluctance to enforce the statutes since our lifestyle habits were continuously changing. Sundays in those years were delightfully quiet. No one mowed grass or did work that made noise. Sunday was considered a time to give thanks, relax, and reflect, just like portrayed on the Andy Griffith Show. The stand-down time was good for us, and I miss it.

Other Places and Things
The Bakeries

Charlotte had a dozen or so neighborhood bakeries. In the fifties supermarkets did not have the kinds of bakery facilities of today. About a dozen commercial bakeries were scattered about the city. These were additional to "cracker packers" or snack foods companies: Lance, M & T, and Swinson Products. Depending on prevailing winds, they made wonderful sensory contributions to the pleasures of childhood. Whether out playing with friends, flying my models around the neighborhood, or riding with my father, nothing could compare with the tantalizing aroma of fresh baked goodies. Queen Pie Company was at 1212 Central Avenue. Its brick building was distinguished by rounded, stacked brick header courses at each corner, that now houses an Irish pub. Griffin Pie was nearby at 933 Louise Avenue. Griffin Pie is remembered for its fried pies in sealed wax paper envelopes (wrappers). The contemporary offerings of fired pies, if one can find them, are nothing like the originals. Patsy Kinsey lived on Central Avenue only a few doors away from Queen Pie and remembers the sweet fragrances from each bakery. Carolina Foods was at 509 36th Street and teased the senses in the northern section of the city.

Charlotte Bread at 1807 South Tryon is quite memorable since we drove by it so many times. Until it relocated to the south of Charlotte to a larger facility, Carolina Foods occupied most of the block. For decades its wonderful aroma was there for all who drove past. In the fifties Mother's Golden Crust bread was its flagship product. The site is a premium location for new development in the South End. The original building of bricks with four faux columns on its façade remains for now. No doubt if one were to carefully sandblast away decades of thick masonry paint on its exposed north facing side, there would be the original facsimile of a loaf of Mother's Bread.

Chapter 7 - Schools, Churches, and Other Places

A&P Bakery, and for a time its offices, was at 822 West Hill Street (now Westmere Avenue) in the classic industrial age building that has been repurposed. I could not smell it from afar, but I knew about its products. So did Melvin Carson, Harding Class of 1957. His mother worked at the bakery. When cakes were not satisfactory formed or iced, they were rejected. Melvin ate a lot of bakery rejects. In the early sixties I worked at the Freedom Drive A & P supermarket, now a Family Dollar Store. We were the first stop for the delivery trucks distributing fresh baked goods. A.G. Boone and G& H Transit were dedicated truck lines for A & P. G & H was headquartered in the office complex that is now Noble Smoke Restaurant on Freedom Drive.

On Friday night after closing a bakery truck arrived. Somehow, each Friday, one of the delicious two-layer iced vanilla cakes arrived with a damaged box. The only appropriate action was for the bagging/stocking staff to promptly liquidate the damaged goods with plenty of chocolate milk. We, of course, had to pay for the milk.

In the fork of the roads between Tuckasegee and Berryhill Roads is a buff-colored brick building that once was Colonial Bakery. The bakery of course served Colonial Stores supermarkets. From our duplex on Marlowe Ave, I could see the building from late fall to mid-spring each year. On days with a steady northerly wind the wonderful smells coming from within would waft three-fourths of a mile to our front door. The building is still extant at this writing and may be subject of a repurposing project.

Merita Bakery (American Bakery) was at 1310 West Trade, in the heart of the Harding neighborhood and near Five Points where Johnson C. Smith is located. Ginny Holden lived a few blocks away. Each year her mother ordered "red and green" bread to make Christmas sandwiches. The Merita Grill across the street was a popular eatery and the site of a notorious murder.

Merita Grill was the scene of a "jack in the box" murder on January 3, 1956. Francis Taylor finished her shift at a restaurant on North Graham Street. Unknown to her, Thomas "Shorty" Taylor, her husband was hidden in her vehicle's trunk.

She left her place of work and after a while stopped in a lot close to Merita Grill, where a man got into the vehicle. "Shorty" heard voices and sounds of two people kissing. Thomas used a screwdriver to open the trunk (no emergency releases in those days), then got out carrying a combination rifle/shotgun, the shells for which he had purchased the previous day. The man in the car got out of the vehicle but was shot and killed. Thomas was found guilty of murder. Apparently, a new trial was ordered. He was found not guilty by a Lincoln County jury, validating an adage I had heard in the bus garage ready room: never mess with a man's car or his wife.

Memorial Stadium/Park Center

American Legion Memorial Stadium was the city's largest sports venue for years. It was a project of the WPA during the 1930s. In the 1940s ice skating events were held there. For decades it was the home of the NC-SC Shrine Bowl. The stadium was tightly arranged between Park Drive and Armory Drive on Fox Street, which would later become Independence Boulevard (now Charlottetown Avenue). Its open horseshoe end faced the Armory Auditorium, the city's primary auditorium venue. The Armory was destroyed by fire in 1954 and replaced by Park Center, later the Grady Cole Center. The stadium recently had a $40 million renovation and is now a first-class arena.

The stadium and Armory anchored the west end of the long bottom land that paralleled 5th and 7th Streets. Independence Park occupied the eastern end. Harding's home games were always played at Memorial. For many years there were large crowds at Friday evening games because they were the only fall sporting events. Attending a game on a pleasant fall evening was a sensory overload for me. Bright lights, acoustics different from anywhere else, the smell of nearby coal burning furnaces mixing with the smell of food wafting through the cool evening air in the stadium. The Shrine Bowl was played to a packed audience the first Saturday of each December and downtown was heavily congested and packed with shoppers. Bryant Park on West Morehead was another WPA project of the 1930s. When Harry P. Harding retired as superintendent of schools in 1949, his retirement event was held in Memorial Stadium.

Auditorium/Coliseum

David Ovens Auditorium and the Charlotte Coliseum (2700 East Independence Boulevard) opened in 1955 and gave Charlotte a first-class

Chapter 7 - Schools, Churches, and Other Places

venue for music/arts/sporting events. The coliseum outlived Charlotte's newer second coliseum which was imploded in 2007. It is presently known as Bojangles Coliseum. When constructed, the Coliseum had the largest unsupported dome of its kind in the world. My only visits there were to the circus and to the roller derby! It was the Charlotte home for Ringling Bros circus for decades. Ovens turned out to be a timely replacement for the Armory Auditorium. For many summers it featured plays and entertainer performances. I remember it most for my high school graduation ceremony.

The Pools

The city maintained three large swimming pool complexes for the public: Cordelia Park on North Davidson, Double Oaks on Statesville Avenue, and Revolution Park at Remount Road and Baringer Drive (also a WPA project). Double Oaks was for Black citizens, Cordelia and Revolution for whites. An updated Cordelia survives today, and the Double Oaks Family Aquatic Center now resides on the former farmland of my aunt and uncle Richard and Janie Carter at 2014 Statesville Avenue.

I knew of no one in Charotte with a pool at their home and I did not stay in a hotel with a pool until many years later. My father took me to Revolution Pool on a few occasions as it was only five blocks away from our home. Our visits were limited depending on polio outbreaks. I returned a couple of times in the 1960s but never hung out there. In earlier years some of my friends walked miles to get there. With a snack bar and miniature golf course across Remount Road it could be an all-day adventure, likewise for the other pools. The #9 Wilmore bus route served Revolution, so it was a regional pool and well populated.

Clark Griffith Park

The Charlotte Hornets baseball team was a farm club of the Washington Senators, and its stadium was named for the owner (until 1955) of the Senators. It was at the end of Meacham Street off South Boulevard I went there several times. It had a long center field, something over 400 feet. It later became Jim Crockett Park. Bob Allison of the Washington Senators/Minnesota Twins signed with the Senators in 1955 and spent his 1956 season with the Hornets, finally making it to Washington in 1958.

Freedom Park/Charlotte Nature Museum

The Nature Museum was and is adjacent to Freedom Park and opened sometime in the 1950s. It was the only nature place in Charlotte and had a small planetarium. I believe every elementary school child of my era visited the Museum on at least one official school trip. It was conveniently located in a sylvan setting. Freedom Park was built to honor WWII service personnel. President Eisenhower spoke at the park's amphitheater during his 1954 visit to Charlotte. In the early sixties a 2-8-0 stream locomotive, an M-41 Walker Bulldog tank, and an F-86 Sabre Jet were added to the park. Only the loco remains today. As quaint as it may seem today, my family would pack a Sunday picnic lunch and head to the park for sun and open air. Later in the 1960s Charlotte Motor Speedway acquired a Cheetah as mascot and it spent most of its time inside a large pen on the Museum grounds. There was a lot of "parking" going on in the parking lots at night. The park's caretaker lived with his wife at the park office on Lilac Road. Shortly before 10:30 the caretaker would announce through a loudspeaker system that the park would close at 10:30. Guys, with their girlfriends close by their sides, would start their cars and vamoose into the darkness of the evening.

Smitty's Beach

Western Mecklenburg was like another county to me. Lots of country roads and fields and woods. Sunday afternoons would find my girlfriend and me cruising around the land west of the airport. Near the Catawba River was Shopton Road West that crossed Wither's Cove at Wither's Bridge. Just to the south side of the bridge was Smitty's Beach owned and managed by a gentleman named Wilbur C. Smith. It was a small but sandy replication of the Carolina coast, a family-centered seasonal venue offering an easy one-day beach adventure, albeit without waves. I did not have a chance to visit there but from the road it looked inviting. A June of 1965 *Charlotte Observer* announcement noted the sale of all the equipment used at the beach would be auctioned following the owner's recent passing.

Racing - Shuffletown/Charlotte Motor Speedway

In the 1950s "racing" usually applied to several small dirt racetracks and

Chapter 7 - Schools, Churches, and Other Places

a few larger paved tracks. The one and three-eighths mile paved Darlington Speedway was the largest of the NASCAR tracks. Racing often meant drag racing at a place whose name was lost in the past. Shuffletown Dragstrip was at a location on NC 16 not far from the Catawba River. It was the era of street muscle cars and drag races were popular both at Shuffletown, and at Concord Dragway which was a classic one-quarter mile strip. Impromptu drag races were frequent on city streets. Challenges of honor were likely to be seen on Independence Boulevard because it had long straights between traffic signals.

To show what one's car could do or to settle a debate among friends, Shuffletown Drag Strip was only a short drive out NC 16. Concord Drag Strip was also quite popular and had bigger named drivers. In 1958, 59 and 60, Chevrolets were the most common hot street cars. Other than 389 Pontiacs there were not many vehicles out there that could handle a 348 Cu. In. Chevy, especially with when equipped with three duces and a four-speed transmission. 410 Edsels were around but rare and no one I knew had ever seen a 430 Super Marauder Mercury. It turns out in the summer of 1960, someone in a Ford Starliner (called the Mystery Ford) with Ford's new but quite rare high performance 352 engine started ripping up Chevys at Concord. The odds of a Chevy driver encountering a Dodge D-500, Chrysler 300, or Plymouth with a cross-ram intake manifold 361 were very slim indeed. Chevys usually ruled the street scene.

I never thought of trying to race anyone in my 130 HP 1954 Ford. It has lost so much compression it probably made only 100 horses. My high school friend Glenn Hipps also had a 1954 Ford, a four door Custom Line with straight drive (manual transmission). He had a novel idea. One evening at The King he proudly drove through, cutting as we called it, with his "stock class" emblazoned on his windshield. He had been to Shuffletown where there were no other vehicles in his class, so he ran the strip, and they gave him a pink slip with his terminal speed and E.T. (elapsed time)! In the strictest sense, he won his class.

Charlotte Motor Speedway was the third of the big tracks behind Darlington and Daytona. It opened in 1960 featuring World 600. The track was beset by construction difficulties and then years of financial stress. The track was built on a site under which there was a significant amount of igneous rock, and it took years to clear it and began to move toward the facility that exists today. In the first 600 the track surface began to break late in the race. Jack Smith was leading in a Pontiac, but his fuel tank took a direct hit from a chunk of bituminous pavement and Joe Lee Johnson won in a Chevrolet. Misfortune plagued the track. The next year driver Reds Cagle drove his 1961 Ford into the single guard rail above a turn. The rail apparently separated at a joint and went through the car causing Cagle to lose a leg. In 1964, World 600 Fireball Roberts' car hit an opening in the back stretch wall and exploded. Roberts died days later. In October that year driver Jimmy Pardue died testing tires when a tire failure sent his car some 200 feet outside the track.

    I went to the 1963 World 600 with my girlfriend and her father. There were far fewer grandstand seats, so we sat in chairs on the second turn. We were covered with dirt and rubber particles near the end of the race. We tried to check track positions with a radio but to no avail. In the final laps Junior Johnson was leading when his 427 Chevrolet blew an engine and Ford jockey Fred Lorenzen won. Charitably speaking Chevrolet fans, some of whom were less than sober, were angry and we were in a 1962 Ford Galaxie 500/XL. It was time to leave. I was a car guy but nothing about the day was fun for me.

Chapter Notes

Racing: Automobile track racing, meaning NASCAR, was indeed a southern sport. NASCAR stock car racing began in the south. Its first "stock car" race was in 1949 and purportedly at the Charlotte Speedway near Little Rock Road and present-day Interstate 85. At the time, vehicle owners were loyal to their brands of cars, not to celebrity drivers.

Race vehicles were fundamentally factory stock cars with a level of builder expertise that made the differences between the participants. Anyone could order a car capable of being transformed into a NASCAR racer. There were no carburetor restrictor plates or body panel templates to ensure managed competition. To quote an old saying: "You run what you brung", was the operative phrase. If your car was slower, you lost. To some degree the factory teams benefited from their factory relationships and track performance proved it. Holman-Moody of Charlotte was a Ford factory team builder. They were located near the original airport fire department in the 1950s/1960s. Charlotte Motor Speedway (original name) was the third big NASCAR oval.

The Automotive Manufacturers Association put forth a resolution in 1957 calling for the de-emphasizing of performance and racing in advertising. Ford, GM and Chrysler signed the document. It changed nothing at GM. Ford, much to its regret, cataloged no real performance engines in 1958 and 1959. The optional big 430 Lincoln power plant gave Thunderbirds some track respectability. By the early 1960s very potent engines from most brands were available again to anyone with cash to order one from a dealer. Supremacy on the big tracks moved back and forth between makes, Pontiac in the early 1960s, Ford for several years. Chrysler with its "Mopars" (lighter weight intermediates - Dodge Coronet and Plymouth Fury) were serious dragstrip contenders for several years in the early-mid-sixties. Chrysler reintroduced its "Hemi" at 426 cubic inch displacement and was a potent NASCAR contender. The introduction of the Pontiac GTO in 1964 began a new era of street muscle cars that lasted until the early 1970s when fuel economy, higher gasoline prices, and surging insurance rates ended the saga.

Park Center. A new venue under construction. When the Armory Auditorium burned in the mid-1950s a new public arena was soon under construction – Park Center in the same location on Kings Drive (formerly Cecil Street and now Pease Lane). American Legion memorial Stadium was located behind the site. Its name was later changed to honor radio personality Grady Cole. The homes seen in the background, which were demolished in the 1960s for the building of Central Piedmont Community College, were on Park Drive, now called Sam Ryburn Walk. Photo: Robinson Spangler Carolina Room, Public Library of Charlotte- Mecklenburg County.

David Ovens Auditorium was completed concurrently with the original Charlotte Coliseum on Independence Blvd. in 1955. It became the city's premiere event venue. Photo: Robinson Spangler Carolina Room, Public Library of Charlotte-Mecklenburg County.

Second Ward High School. The many school buildings built in the 1920s and 1930s were quite similar – one multiple story structure housing most if not all functions. Auditoriums were typically a prominent façade, often at one end of a structure. Tall windows, high ceilings, steam heated cast iron radiators, doors with operating transoms above for ventilation were characteristic attributes of the times. A more recent addition is visible at right, and it is entirely different from the style and materials of the pre-WWII era. Photo: Robinson Spangler Carolina Room, Public Library of Charlotte- Mecklenburg County.

Herbert Spaugh Junior High School – now Bishop Spaugh Administrative Center. Opened in 1957, this was my junior high school. I had World History in the classroom at the right end of this building. Most schools of the period were sprawling, single story, structurally expressive, and minimalist in appearance. Something like ranch houses of the education world. Architecturally, it was the beginning of the George Jetson era. The remaining earlier schools with their brick facades and classic features have been more durable. Google photo.

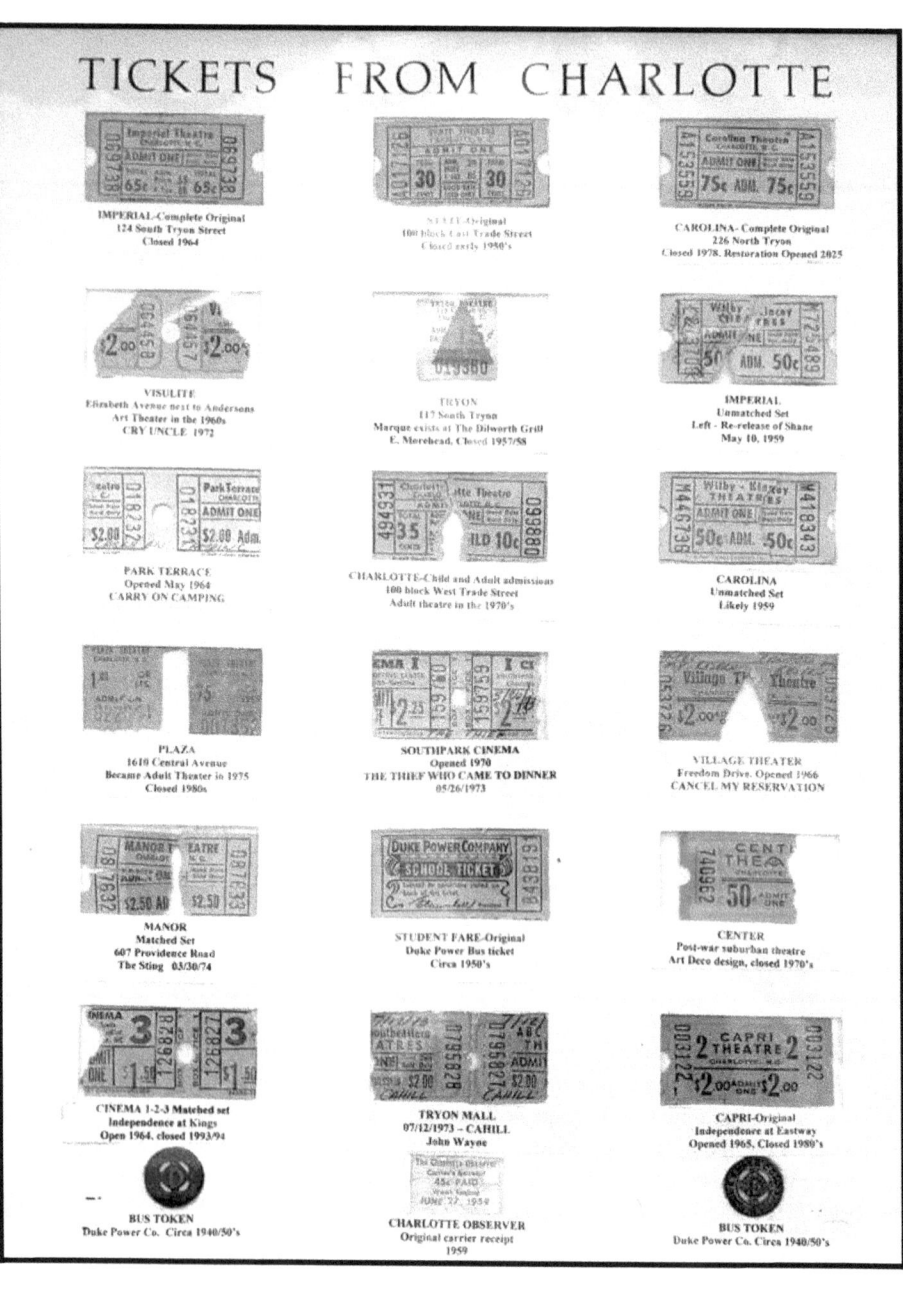

Movie Tickets from Charlotte Movie Theaters. Torn tickets stubs including the intact State Theater ticket. Photo: The Author's Ticket Collection.

Chapter 8
Movies and Other Things

My Favorite Places – The Theaters

Having captured the nation during the depression, movies uplifted it in WWII and then just keep rolling into the 1950s. Fact is, as I was growing up going to a "show" was the biggest deal of deals for me. Television did not affect my movie going since we had no TV until 1959. I watched the array of late fifties westerns on my grandmother's TV on weekends, but they could not compete with the adventures of Randolph Scott or John Wayne films. Based on declining theater attendance, many Americans thought otherwise. I saw lots of movies. That luxury continued even into high school when I had a girlfriend to join me.

Charlotte had four groups of theaters extant in the period of our journey. Three pre-dated talkies (with prior names) and survived for decades. The first group were the most prestigious and upscale and always had first run features. The Carolina (226 North Tryon), Imperial (124 South Tryon), and Dilworth (1607 South Boulevard) were part of Wilby-Kincey Corp. and were well known. Broadway at 209 South Tryon suffered a fire in the early 1950s and reopened for a short time as the Fox before closing in 1959. The Manor (607) Providence Road and the art deco Center (1427 East Morehead) were upscale neighborhood houses and part of Steward Everett Theaters. Both were in classier areas; the Manor in Myers Park and the Center on East Morehead close to Queens Road near Charlotte Memorial Hospital (now Atrium).

Next, we have the neighborhood group. The Plaza at 1610 in Midwood was a neighborhood venue with first run films. The Visulite at 1615 Elizabeth Avenue served the Elizabeth neighborhood and was in the shadow of Presbyterian Hospital (Novant). The Astor at 511 East 36th Street was "North Charlotte's" theater and had a checkered history. It is now a neighborhood events venue. The newest, Belvedere (2738 Rozzells Ferry Road), was a loner of sorts and figuratively was in the middle of nowhere but prospered for a while.

The next group was the uptown "second run" theaters: Charlotte at

123 West Trade, State at 122 East Trade, and Tryon at 117 South Tryon. The third group was the Black theaters: Grand, (333 Beatties Ford Road), Lincoln (408 East Second Street), and Savoy (508 South McDowell Street) in Second Ward (Brooklyn). In 1961/62 The Ritz opened at 1201 Beattie's Ford Road.

The fourth group was the drive-in theaters: South 29 Drive-In, North 29 Drive-In, York Road Drive-In, Statesville Road Drive-In, Thrift Road Drive-In (later known as West 16), Albemarle Road Drive-In, Pineville Road Drive-In, and Monroe Road Drive-In. Unique to movie houses was the little-known Morris Field Theater that closed after WWII and was heavily dependent on military personnel during WWII. It then reopened for a short while. It was quite simplistic – a building with rows of chairs and a projection booth.

The Manor survived as a theater until 2020. It was a cell in a multiple tenant strip center and its marquee is still in place. The Carolina has been magnificently restored and reopened as part of an urban project. Its façade was saved, stored, and has been reassembled inside the main project hotel lobby to become part of the completed project. The grand building survives and is designated as a historic landmark. The Charlotte closed long ago and later became a Hooters Restaurant on West Trade Street, which remained open until its closure in 2024. The Astor is now a neighborhood playhouse with its original marquee. The Visulite building survives and hosts events, also with its original marquee. The Belvedere building also survives, and it is a dental clinic. The Ritz site is now a public gathering open space in remembrance of the theatre. Everything else is gone with one exception. The Dilworth Grill on East Morehead at South McDowell is the second home for the theater marquee that graced the Tryon until it closed in 1958.

Carolina dated to 1927 and was the largest, most ornate followed by the Imperial. Both were multiple level theaters. My first visit to Carolina may have been on June 19, 1953. Dean Martin and Jerry Lewis were starring in *Scared Stiff*. My father drove uptown and as always, he listened to news programs. We parked on North College Street. The commentator was describing the executions of Julius and Ethel Rosenberg. It was the time of the "Red Scare" and the Rosenbergs' had been convicted of espionage. Carolina was the usual venue for Martin and Lewis movies. I saw many great

Chapter 8 - Movies and Other Things

films there: *Mr. Roberts* (1955 Henry Fonda & Jack Lemmond), the epic John Ford classic *The Searchers* (1956 John Wayne), *Rio Bravo* (1959 John Wayne, Dean Martin, & Rick Nelson), *You're Never Too Young* (1955 Dean Martin and Jerry Lewis), *A Summer Place* (1959 Troy Donohue & Sandra Dee). Both *Giant* (Rock Hudson and Elizabeth Taylor 1956) and *Peyton Place* (1957 Lana Turner and Hope Lange) also played Carolina. Elvis Pressley appeared on stage there in 1956.

Generally, Carolina ran the biggest films. In 1962 it was renovated to show films in the new Cinerama format. Projection and sound technology went through several improvements in the 1950s such as CinemaScope, the first film of which was *The Robe* that played there in 1953. The films I saw after the Cinerama renovation were *The Longest Day* and *How the West Was Won* each in 1963. The sound was outstanding. *The Sound of Music* was released in 1965, Carolina booked it. However, it may have been the grand finale for Carolina. Cinerama faded as did downtown attendance. The last film I saw there was with my wife, Emily, in the summer of 1972, Jennifer O'Neill in *Summer of '42*. Not long afterwards Carolina became a martial arts movie house and finally closed in 1978. In early 2025, Carolina reopened with all the splendid opulence of its 1927 iteration.

The Imperial was Wilby-Kincey's corresponding house on South Tryon. It seemed to have more western and adventure films, still first runs, so with one block less to walk my feet tended to deliver me there. Like Carolina, it had a long, narrow lobby that emptied into its auditorium, which also like Carolina was quite high above its stage. Its manager for years was Glenn Grove, and he ran a tight operation. Carolina and Imperial had uniformed ushers. If there was chatter in the auditorium, an usher would arrive at the row of the offender(s) and a flashlight beam would signal for quiet. Imperial's big hauls: *Trapeze* (1955 Bert Lancaster & Tony Curtis), *The Ten Commandments* (1956 Yul Brenner, Anne Baxter & Yvonne De Carlo), *Night of The Hunter* (1955 Robert Mitchum & Shelley Winters), and *Marty* (1956 Ernest Borgnine and Betsy Blair).

When Imperial showed *The Thing from Outer Space*, its *Charlotte Observer* ad cautioned a nurse would be on duty for those faint of heart. My first experience with 3-D movies was at the Imperial, probably *Hondo*. The cardboard and acetate glasses required for 3-D and the film format itself went away in only a few years. The final film I saw at Imperial was *PT-109* starring Cliff Robertson in 1963. Imperial closed in 1964 and was replaced by Park Terrace at Park Road Shopping Center. The First Citizens Building occupies the site now.

The Manor was in a pricier part of the city and required a bus transfer to get there. Consequently, I did not visit there as often. Among its many hit films was the 1956 blockbuster, not shown until September 1957, *Around the World in Eighty Days* (David Niven, Cantinflas, and Shirley MacLaine).

The Center was the other Stewart and Everett's theater. It was an eclectic design, the interior of which had its stairways to the upper vestibule adorned with mirrors. The mirrors and railings were very much art deco. It took a bus transfer to get there, and it was a short ride. The Center showed many features that captured my interest. The first film I recall there was *Sabre Jet* (Robert Stack, Coleen Gray, Leon Ames). The film was released in September 1953 just after the Korean War Armistice. It was a good action film for the time with lots of flying. In the red scare era of Senator Joe McCarthy, it had lots of appeal. F-86s were powered by GE J-47 jet engines, an example of which was on a mobile stand in front of the box office. No further inducement was needed. At the time, I was barely into plastic model airplanes, but I am sure the next day I was flying something around our backyard bombing commies!

The original *3:10 To Yuma* (Glenn Ford, Van Heflin, Flecia Farr) of 1957 was a memorable film at the Center. The Center's big catch was the epic *Spartacus* (Kirk Douglas and Jean Simmons in 1960). Two friends and I went to an evening show in 1961 knowing the last #3 bus to the square would turn from Kenilworth onto Morehead at about 11:15 p.m. The film was long and at about 11:05 p.m. panic set in. No option but to leave. We backed up the aisle to catch every glimpse of action. We hit the lobby and ran out the doors and as fast as we could, then sprinted the long block uphill to Kenilworth. The bus arrived within a minute of our arrival. We were home safely by 11:55 p.m.

The Center had relied on adjacent lots for parking and for some reason it did not benefit from proximity to wealthier areas as did the Manor. The last film I saw there was *This Property Is Condemned* in 1966 and based on a Tennessee Wiliams play, well-acted by Natalie Wood but depressing. The

Chapter 8 - Movies and Other Things

Center declined and closed in 1977.

Dilworth was not as large as Carolina or Imperial but entirely adequate for a neighborhood movie house. It reflected the character of the area and was nested among Dilworth Pharmacy, a grocery store, a bank, and a bakery. I am sure my father and I visited there many times but can only recall two films before I graduated. *A Yank in the RAF* (Tyrone Power and Betty Grable) was a 1941 pre-war movie that I found disappointing. It was mostly a love story and had little flying action – a swindle I thought.

The other film was *Key Largo* (Humphrey Bogart and Edward G. Robinson), a re-run from 1948. Dilworth was still trying to be a first-run theatre. Dilworth scored big when in 1962, *Cleopatra* (/Richard Burton and Elizabeth Taylor) began its long run there. It was all but necessary to order tickets by mail for the film that opened on June 26, 1963. It also ran the Sophia Loren classic *Yesterday, Today, and Tomorrow*. The last film I saw there was probably *Major Dundee* (1965 Charlton Heston). Dilworth was a first-run house for some years then declined. It was destroyed by fire in January of 1984.

Plaza was the Midwood neighborhood theater equivalent to Dilworth. It was of art deco style and part of the business strip between Pecan Avenue and The Plaza. It required a bus transfer and was beyond my range. It began a decline in the seventies, first by showing "soft core" adult features, then becoming a full adult house. Interestingly, on June 17, 1970, I had a double date, my side of which was blind, and the movie was *The Cheyenne Social Club* (James Stewart and Henry Fonda), just released that very week. Two days later I asked the lovely lady who was my date to marry me, and she said yes.

The Plaza became the Pussycat adult theater in 1975 and languished as such into the eighties. Interestingly in the context of the times, an adult theater sometimes became a curiosity rather than pariah. An administrative assistant (they were called secretaries then) at the architectural firm at which I worked purchased a Pussycat membership as a lark for one of our executives. The Plaza was eventually demolished, and a bank resides in its approximate location now.

The Visulite was a unique place. It like Plaza and Dilworth was a pre-war movie house and. I remember well seeing *The Fastest Gun Alive* (Glenn

Ford and Broderick Crawford). It was a very good but forgotten western. It was released in 1956. In the early sixties Visulite became an "art" theater. There was a public flap about the appropriateness of the film titled *For Members Only*. Then in 1964 Visulite presented Ian Flemming's *Goldfinger* and continued into the 1970s as a first run house. Today it is a community event house, its marquee still in place.

The Belvedere was the city's newest theater, until the Ritz opened 1961/62 and Charlottetown I & II opened in 1963. The *Charlotte Observer* featured its opening day – December 25, 1950 (there is still a website incorrectly noting its opening in 1955). Its visual presentation was imposing — that of an Egyptian citadel overlooking the Nile. My father took me there once and even then, I sensed it was an odd location for a movie house. The Smallwood and Wesley Heights neighborhoods were close by to support it. However, the theater did not have the benefit of nearby businesses and people activities of the sort that surrounded Manor, Center and Visulite. Its abstruse ambience made it seem like an outlier to me. It was successful for many years. There was a narrative, later corrected, that the Belvedere was a Black theater in a Black neighborhood. The surrounding neighborhoods were of course White. Black theaters were sometimes omitted in the local newspaper movie pages, or they were text listings in Sunday editions, or for a time grouped separately. Belvedere was always congregated with the White theaters. In retrospect it is curious to me why someone wanted to build it at that location. The building is now a dental clinic.

The State was an old movie house and was on its third or fourth name by 1950. It had become a second run house and although I saw westerns there with my dad, I can recall no titles. The State was the first downtown casualty of the TV era impacts on theaters. I suspect parking was also a factor. State had closed by the time I was free to roam at 10 years old. Fortunately, I have an untorn State ticket in my collection.

Broadway, and later Fox, is a distant memory for me. Broadway was a pre-1920s theater. My dad took me there to see a movie about Blackbeard the pirate. I recall only Blackbeard being buried in sand up to his neck and the surf coming in. It was damaged by fire in the mid-1950s, and it was closed for some time. It reopened as the Fox. I did not visit there again and I'm not certain why. Fox closed about 1958/59 when demolition begin for

Chapter 8 - Movies and Other Things

the Cutter Building (later American Credit, then Barclays, now 201 South Tryon).

Tryon was my default movie house. It was in the center of things, close to Tanner's, and convenient to S.H. Kress. When you are 10-12 those things are paramount. For eating efficiency Tryon's popcorn came in tall bags rather than boxes. By the end of the second feature, it would be time for a Snickers bar which provided protein along with its sugar. On weekends Tryon always had three features, usually one or two cartoons, and frequently a Three Stooges or Joe McDoakes short. Its first feature began at 10:00 a.m. or shortly afterwards. A primary feature, two cartoons, perhaps a Bowery Boys film, and a Tim Holt western plus a stooge would yield about 3 hours and 30 Minutes of solid entertainment. That would put me on the street between 1:30 p.m. and 1:45 p.m. and in time for a late lunch at Tanner's at 123 South Tryon. A few times my father would bring me a cheeseburger and punch so I could remain in the movie house and enjoy my lunch. What a deal. A typical Saturday offering on June 1, 1957: the features were: Glenn Ford in *The Fastest Gun Alive*, the Bowery Boys in *Crashing Las Vegas*, and *Earth vs. Flying Saucers* plus a cartoon. As attendance declined, Tryon began showing more films with adult themes during the week. Tryon closed in 1958 and left the downtown market for second runs to the Charlotte Theatre. Stand there today and look up, one will see 503 feet of One South at The Plaza.

Charlotte Theater's ambience was basic indeed. What class it had was in its bright marquee. Its movie offerings were the same as Tryon, but it was a simply square tube building between West Trade and the alley behind. Its air conditioning was questionable, and it generally had the smell of soft drink syrup. Of course, at the time movie patrons left their cups, popcorn boxes, and candy wrappers on the floors. Charlotte was old. Nevertheless, I saw many films there. At some point *Colt 45* starring Charlotte's Randolph Scott, was featured there. It may have been Charlotte's only first run in years. The candy case of its small lobby was filled with an assortment of pistols to promote the film. Miller's Central Hat Shop was next door.

Once in junior high school, I felt more adult, and Charlotte simply did not fit my newfound sense of being. I think I saw my last film there around 1956/57. The Charlotte had the distinction, or perhaps notoriety, in its final years of being the only downtown theater to become an adult house and held on a few years in part because office workers, usually small groups of men and women, would drop in for long lunch hours. The Charlotte closed in the 1980's.

Astor theater was way out of my travel range although my father's No. 6 Elizabeth-North Charlotte route took me past the Astor many times. I do not recall when it closed, however, it was reopened as an adult theater and was active as such in 1966 and at least through 1974 before closing again. The building was used by a church for a while. It was a long drive from our home and the former mill village area was in a slow decline. My father never took me there. The area, now known as NoDa, is booming with new growth and Astor is a neighborhood playhouse.

Davidson and Pineville purportedly had movie theaters, but they are outside our scope. One forgotten theater prospered for a short time during WWII – the Morris Field Theater. Located at 65 Morris Field Drive between what is now Billy Graham Parkway and the former terminal/base operations, it was an amenity primarily dependent on the military base population and was a building with non-fixed seating. Ads appeared in the *Charlotte Observer* in mid-1947 and apparently the operation shut down afterwards as the base effectively closed. It reopened again and was listed in the city directories in 1951 but was not listed in 1952 or 1953.

The passing of downtown theaters began with the loss of the State. Five years later the Tryon and Fox had closed. The Imperial and Carolina carried the demand but when Park Terrace opened in 1964 the Imperial closed, and it was only a matter of time. At the very end of 1963 the Charlottetown Cinema I & II opened and changed everything. Capri gave East Independence a top-drawer movie house (*The Lion in Winter* and *Poseidon Adventure*). The opening of the Village at Freedom Village in 1966 finally did the same for the westside (it featured the colossal hit *Airport* in 1970"). The historic Grand Theater closed about 1967, and its building survives.

It was wonderful to be in a theater on Friday evening watching Randolph Scott dispatch bad guys and knowing the next morning I would be riding around our backyard on my imaginary horse, complete with my requisite twin-holstered cap pistols, and replicating the adventures I had seen on the big screen. Once the Tryon closed options became limited, but my interests had changed to more mature stories usually seen at the Imperial, Carolina,

Chapter 8 - Movies and Other Things

Center, or Manor.

My favorite character films: Gary Cooper in *High Noon* (Imperial), Van Heflin/Glenn Ford in *3:10 to Yuma* (Center), John Wayne in *The Searchers* (Carolina), and Cary Grant in *North by Northwest* (probably Manor). Here are some of the most memorable films: 1950 – 1963: *The Thing from Outer Space, Bridges at Toko-Ri, You're Never Too Young, Gunfight at OK Corral, Rio Bravo, A Summer Place, North by Northwest, The Longest Day, Seven Men from Now, Dial M for Murder, Ride The High Country, The Far Country, The Man Who Shot Liberty Valance, Charade,* and *Rear Window.*

Lifestyles - Radio, and Becoming a "Ham"

The importance of radio in the 1950s may be difficult to grasp in today's digital universe. My father listened to news and commentaries. There was more than enough news during the Korean War (June 25, 1950 – July 27, 1953) and the concurrent "red scare". The city's radio stations were: 1110 WBT – CBS; 1240 WSOC – NBC; 930 WIST - Mutual; 610 WAYS – ABC; 1600 WGIV – Unaffiliated, 1480 WWOK - Unaffiliated. In the late 1950s WKTC at 1310 entered the market and became the city's dedicated country music station. "Big WAYS", WIST (Fabulous Forty), and WWOK (Vinnie Vincent) were the rock and pop stations. WBT was a 50,000 watt "clear channel station". Its original home was the Wilder Building at South Tryon and East Third. In the mid-fifties Jefferson Standard Broadcasting moved to a dedicated building at One Julian Price Place overlooking Bryant Park (J.N. Pease designed the building). WGIV, at 700 Remount Road at the corner of Toomey Avenue, targeted Black audiences and had the notable personalities Joy Boy Sanders, Genial Gene, Chatty Hattie, and Rocking Ray Gooding. Many of us listened to WGIV, especially a crossover DJ named Pete Toomey. Rocking Ray was a popular guest DJ at functions including Harding's 1983 reunion event.

The pop stations were an essential part of our culture since there were no mobile phones, no Spotify, or other ways to hear music except for records. Eight-track cartridges were a mid-sixties creation and first appeared in vehicles in 1966. Audio cassettes were several years later. Portable radios were popular. However, they required one or more batteries that could be depleted during an afternoon picnic. I saw my first transistor radio in 1959.

Many were pocket sized and required only a small battery which had a much longer service life.

Later into the fifties and sixties radio dials had small triangle symbols at the 640 and 1240 frequencies. This was part of our cold war posture, and all commercial broadcasts were to shut down in case of Soviet Union attack. The 640 and 1240 frequencies would provide US government information to citizens. It took television about a decade to supplant radio as a primary source of news, weather, sports, and commentary. It is easy to follow the changes by looking at radio schedules. *The Lone Ranger* and *Sgt. Preston of the Yukon* were two of my favorite radio shows. Radio dramas are terrific for stimulating one's imagination. Television ended all that rather quickly. In fact, *The Lone Ranger* was on both radio and television for a time. I listened to *The Lone Ranger* in late afternoon trips with my father for groceries, etc. If I had to select influential forces in my childhood development *The Lone Ranger* would be at the top.

Speaking of radio, when I was twelve, one of my grandmother's nephews, Bill Rollins, lived at her house as a roomer for about a year. He was a draftsman and an amateur radio operator or "ham" as they were known. He became my technology mentor. Amateur radio was a popular avocation. It was an early form of social media based on one's skills/interest with radio technology. Amateurs were from all employments/professions and shared an interest in building and operating radio communications. In parts of the world where communications were sketchy or did not exist, amateur radio was invaluable, especially in times of natural disasters.

To become an amateur radio operator, it was necessary to be licensed by the FCC since hams used designated frequencies regulated by the federal government. With a lot of tutoring from my grandmother's boarder, I obtained an FCC license in April 1958 when I was twelve. My call sign was "KN4VAW". It was a "novice" grade license as denoted by the "N" which restricted me to using Morse code rather than voice transmissions. I built my own transmitter and have a parts receipt from Dixie Radio for $12.58. I operated in the 80-meter band on 3730 kilocycles. On my first night of operation, with only 5 watts of signal output, I communicated with a ham in New York state. Moving through junior high school, my interest in radio and electronics was sidetracked, and I did not pursue a general class license which would have enabled me to use voice.

I did have an interest in a related electronics pursuit. 126 West Fifth Street was an unimposing storefront of a place almost forgotten – Joe Little Record Shop/Joe Little Hi-Fi Center. By the time I was fifteen I had an interest in "Hi-Fi", a marker for those who were cool. It was "stereophonic" by then but still went by its former moniker. It was cool to have a Gerrard turntable and some sort of hi-fi sound system. I could afford neither. Friends and I would drop in the Joe Little's and ponder how we could ever afford the Harmon Karden tuners that always played cool music when we visited. Of course, the shop had well designed acoustics, more so than most homes. I had a Voice of Music portable stereo system, basically an attractive box with top and bottom halves, each with a speaker, one with a stackable turntable. One half went to each of two end tables. A simple fader, with bass and treble knobs was all I had. It was a changer equipped so I could load up with ten records. To be cool I needed individual sound components with a single turntable. And no one I knew in high school had that set up. Once fully engaged in classes at Old Harding my hi-fi aspirations melted away. Joe Little's shop was more durable, and he operated it until he retired in 1996.

Chapter Notes

Features: In the early 1950s a full agenda at most theaters began with a newsreel, a narrated two- or three-minutes summary of news events. The Korean War dominated during the 1950 – 1953 years. Newsreels were produced by movie studios with noted narrators like Ed Herlihy (Universal Studios). Although the newsreels continued into the 1960s, they seemed to be fewer in number as the decade progressed, possibly a casualty to TV news. Even as a child I recognized the sensationalistic aspect of their narrative, much like a carnival barker. A color cartoon usually preceded the motion picture itself or "feature" as it was called. If the movie was especially long kids could expect the cartoon to be deleted. Second run theaters such as the Tryon would offer three "features" on Saturdays.

Three Stooges/Joe McDoakes: The Three Stooges made nearly 200 so-called "shorts" that would precede a feature film. Less numerous than Bugs Bunny or Tom and Jerry cartoons, they were a special treat. Usually, about 17 minutes long, they were good fillers for a shorter film when the running cycles for most theaters were about two hours. The first "Stooges" short was filmed in 1934 and final short in 1958 although the trio did several films.

Joe McDoakes was played by George O'Hanlon, and this series of shorts was produced in the 1940s until 1956. McDoakes was always cast as the unluckiest of devoted husbands whose every scheme went sour.

Randolph Scott: Scott was a notable actor whose family lived at the corner of Arosa Avenue and Dilworth Road. The house with its terra cotta roof is still standing. His biography is very much worth reading. He attended UNC-Chapel Hill and in the late 1920s moved to Hollywood. He was a highly regarded actor who excelled in many roles for two decades and then settled into westerns in the 1950s. As the consummate western actor, he was impeccably dressed in the same style hat and always wearing a bandana, and nice leather vest. His comportment was as iconic as that of John Wayne but with sharper looks. For me his most memorable movie was *Seven Men from Now* with Lee Marvin and Don Red Barry. His final film was *Ride the High Country* in 1962 with Joel McCrea. Scott and his wife rest in Elmwood Cemetery on West Sixth Street.

Records: Until the marketing of eight track tapes in the middle 1960s, music was available only on radio, TV, or phonograph records. 78 RPM records were still popular when I was very young but usually had only one song per side. Long-playing 33 1/3 RPM records became the standard in the fifties since eight to twelve average songs could be recorded on each side. Most popular single song releases used "45s" (45 RPM turntable speed) and had a song on each side. Many record players had a device that allowed stacking up to 10 45s, or ten 33s. In the late 1950s 45s were usually priced at $0.98. Extended play 45s with two songs per side were $1.29. Records were sold at many pharmacies, department stores, and record shops. Records of course were the "ammo" that fed thousands of juke boxes across the nation.

State Theater. Just beyond Kress on East Trade was the State Theater. It was an old movie house, known by several previous names, and closed in the early 1950s. It was the first of the uptown movie houses to close in the new era of TV. The movie title on the marquee is not quite legible. Each of the vehicles is pre-1949, one appears to be a 1948 model. The theater's location is approximately at the loading dock entrance ramp of One South at The Plaza (formerly Bank of America Plaza). Photo: Courtesy Charles Spencer Collection.

Tryon Theater. The epicenter of my downtown adventures. St Patrick's Day Parade photo from 1957. The gentleman with the raised arm is WBT radio personality Grady Cole with author Harry Golden, who lived on Elizabeth Avenue, to his left. The Tryon marquee is in the background. It survives, albeit without the "T" at the Dilworth Grill on East Morehead. Three feature films were in play at Tryon. No Tarzan film was showing but rather former Tarzan star himself, Johnny Weismuller, in his final performance as Jungle Jim in *Devil Goddess*. The marquee correctly listed the *East Side Kids* but its Charlotte Observer ad indicated *The Bowery Boys* and, in fact, they were they were the same but had received a name change after the 1943 film was made. *Apache Woman* was a "B" western that starred Lloyd Bridges, father of Jeff Bridges. Photo: Robinson Spangler Carolina Room, Public Library of Charlotte-Mecklenburg County.

Charlotte Theater. Although Charlotte Theatre was an old, second run movie house, its marquee took a back seat to none. Brightly lighted and clearly legible, here announcing Joel McCrea starring in The *Tall Stranger* from 1957. The second feature was a British film *Son of Robin Hood*. Senator John F. Kennedy's motorcade is passing by and heading east on West Trade Street on September 17, during his fall 1960 Presidential campaign. Kennedy is riding in a 1960 Ford Sunliner convertible with a rare optional – a deluxe hood ornament. The other convertible on the right side of the photo is one of the most bizarre, disjointed designs of the "fins" era – a 1961 Plymouth Fury. Visible on the right is the Oriental Restaurant and the Selwyn Hotel, also the location of Bailey's Selwyn Cafeteria. The New Yorker Restaurant sign can be seen beyond the marquee. Photo: Robinson Spangler Carolina Room, Public Library of Charlotte-Mecklenburg County.

Belvedere Theatre at 75. The movie house opened on Christmas Day 1950. The building is now in use as a dental clinic. Its unique facade still conveys that a theater once lived there. A full page of congratulatory messages was offered by various contractors/suppliers in the December 24 *Charlotte Observer*. The theater opened with a Warner Bros. feature film *The Flame and The Arrow* starring Burt Lancaster and Virgina Mayo. Google photo.

The Carolina Theatre – Reborn. It opened before the "talkies" in 1927 and was the class movie house of Charlotte for decades. It closed in 1978. Good fortune was in its path in the form of The Foundation For The Carolinas. After several years of extensive and laborious restoration work, the state-of-the-art Carolina reopened in early 2025 as a multi-function venue. Its grandeur is displayed in this photo taken from the high point of its immense balcony.

Chapter 9
Streetwise – Life Skills and Learning

As fondly as some of my peers think of our past childhoods, the society of the 1950s was not without worry or risks. I was not allowed on the city's streets without some admonition of potential dangers. Fundamental to most of us was: "do not speak with strangers". No one told me why there was danger, but the message carried enough gravitas that I heeded one hundred percent. I was told that if I were being followed, I was to cross the street and return in the direction from which I came. If someone sat down immediately beside me in a movie I should get up, get a soft drink, then sit somewhere else. I learned that if I felt uncomfortable, I should vacate the area of threat. It turned out, I never encountered a situation in which I felt threatened or fearful. We all knew there were strange folks out there in our world but did not understand their motivations or objectives. In hindsight our understanding of the difficulties affecting some people was sketchy and inadequate.

There were dangers to be sure. A broken bone from time to time was about the worst occurrence a child might have. Before the Salk polio vaccine became available in 1955 my biggest fear, and that of many friends, was being confined to an iron lung with polio. That was very real for many of us. There were other horrors. I remember hearing of cases in which a child became locked in an abandoned refrigerator and died. It took such tragedies to finally cause manufacturers to develop locks that could be pushed open from the inside. The story of Joyce and Carl Burns illustrated just how bad things could go wrong.

My activities and adventures took place in an ambient sensory environment unlike that of today. When growing up sounds could be quite helpful. I did not have a watch until I was 10. When we were outside playing, we could usually hear twelve o'clock whistles from one or more manufacturing plants that announced lunch hour. The same whistles sounded return to work time at one o'clock. The eight o'clock morning whistle was of little value to a ten-year-old on a summer vacation day. The five o'clock whistle, especially on shorter days of fall and winter, was a clear signal to return to my grandmother's or to home for dinner. Likewise, the regular passage of city buses told time, especially at night. I had no ear buds to insulate me from the sounds of the city or nature.

I appreciated the danger of speeding vehicles because I was so often a pedestrian. My father gave me some good urban survival pointers. He told me to always stand 3 feet away from the curb when vehicles were present. He also warned me when walking on the edge of a street without a sidewalk I should keep my eyes on the right front tire of any oncoming vehicles rather than the vehicle or driver. I was told never to bend over to pick up anything when a vehicle was around. A basic rule was never to run across any street, always walk. I knew I had to turn around and look before I crossed at an intersection, even if I had a green light. My father told me to motion a turning vehicle onward rather than walk in front of one. I did not have a bike, and I think that relieved my father and grandparents of another worry. No doubt my father had some bus driver friends keeping an eye on me.

By being with my father so often at such a young age I was in proximity to many adults. I heard a lot of things, some of them out of bounds for this narrative and some extremely valuable. There was so much to learn and to see how different people communicated and performed their jobs. It did not take long to assess who knew their stuff and who was fluff. In hindsight, it was more than helpful and was an early education in life skills. Then, as today, to be an expert one needed only to breathe and have a mouth. I thought there were a lot of experts. At ten, eleven, twelve it was obvious to me some folks were clear-minded, deliberate thinkers and others were somewhere else. In later years when working at my uncle's service station I realized "hangers-around" were omni present and had a solution for every perceived grievance. Nothing has changed. Today cell phones and social platforms exponentially expand the universe for lunacy. Facts seldom get in the way of a good emotional outburst. I was fortunate and blessed to have had benefit of some smart, educated, dispassionate people who provided fine examples for my friends and me, especially teachers.

A significant learning experience was the McCarthy era. It was a difficult time for the nation, and it took me a few years to sort things out. Anything that was wrong, went awry, failed to perform as expected, etc. was invariably blamed on "the Communists". There was little question the Soviet Union

(Russia), then as now, was a clear and present danger. Unfortunately, that fed the hysteria promoted by Sen Joseph McCarty of Wisconsin, hence the term McCarthyism. The notable Roy Cohn was McCarthy's henchman. I saw short features at theatres and on television depicting how to recognize communists in our midst. The contemporary and chronic affliction that has caused so many to affix themselves to conspiracy theories is nothing new, only more pernicious now than during the McCarthy era. It is surprising that war babies – the predecessors of the baby boomers - did not grow up with paranoia, and in fact some did. Fortunately, the economic surge of the late fifties helped put minds elsewhere. It was a formative time.

A huge benefit of *Haulin' Around Town* was seeing commerce being conducted. As a child I always listened as children were expected to do just that. I was impressed by those who spoke confidently and kept their cool. Street smart meant listening and learning. While I did not have a regular home as it was, I had opportunities my contemporaries perhaps did not. My career employment benefited from what I heard and learned in those years. Whether in movies, radio/TV, church, school, or elsewhere I had role models who knew how to conduct themselves with character, honor, and class.

Chapter 10
In Retrospect

The years covered by our narrative had generally steady social norms and clearly defined expectations of how children and young adults were to conduct themselves. The period was framed by a benchmark year of 1950 and closed at a point no one would have imagined. The assassination of two Presidents, one being John F. Kennedy, the other Ngo Dinh Diem of South Vietnam, a race to the moon and beyond, a social movement for racial equity, and the beginnings of a war of choice in Southeast Asia that was not required for survival of our democracy, and which afflicted the nation for decades, greeted the war babies and early boomers.

I grew up in a safe environment. Mine was not a typical family but I was neither cold nor hungry due to my supporting family network. Local, state, and especially the federal government that today's critics want to destroy, each engaged to ensure the best educational opportunities were given to students. On a local level, Charlotte and Mecklenburg schools tried to educate all young people. Our segregated system almost certainly created inequalities. However, the focus on education was never in doubt. During this time parents, public school teachers, Sunday school teachers, Scout leaders, and others put forth a collaboration with the same objective - my generation would take advantage of the educational avenues readily available to establish ourselves more successfully than the generation of the Great Depression era and WWII. Preserving those opportunities had been an objective of those who fought WWII. Most citizens seemed to understand and appreciate industry, education, and science that gave the nation so many good things, making life measurably much better than in the depression and earlier decades. It was an era of new and better, and most folks felt good about themselves and their futures. In 2025 there is a measurable ignorance of what got us to the standard of living we have. The combination of artificial intelligence and overwhelming social media consumption will test our national character in ways my generation never imagined.

My classmates and I had Civics in ninth grade. We learned the basics of our republic. My classmates and I understood how our judicial system works. My understanding of the "rule of law", the right to an attorney, and appreciation for our judicial system is directly attributable to Mr. Chuck Burn who once arranged a visit for our class to Mecklenburg Superior Court. We were taught pride in the nation and knowledge about those who researched, discovered, manufactured, built, and put in place so much to make the nation work. We understood that as citizens, my friends and I were expected to compromise for the better good of the nation. Honoring our responsibilities was presented as our obligation. Mr. Douglas Crotts, junior year US History, was exemplary of our parents' generation and made just that point. Crotts was a highly decorated Marine who had walked around the lagoon at Tarawa on November 20, 1943, oblivious to enemy fire, directing vehicles around shell holes under the shallow water's surface. He received his Navy Cross from Adm. Chester Nimitz personally. He never said a word about his experiences to our class. We learned only from his obituary.

Mr. Eugene Todd, a native Charlottean, former Harding student, former Harding instructor, and former CMS principal, was more influential on me and some of my friends than we realized at the time. He often stated that "things evolve". His was clearly an accurate statement. I learned it was ok to question established norms. That of course set into motion a desire "to always get the facts". Mr. Todd made it into 2023. I spoke at his service. After our 2013 reunion Todd and I began having coffee regularly. On the first occasion I apologized for not being a better student. I wanted him to know I recognized how much he cared for us. Always gracious, he stated he knew that Jack (my friend Jack Washam) and I would be ok. That made my day. May God bless all those folks.

The educational narrative of our heritage was always positive, if selectively sanitized. I did not understand that at the time but soon would. As I continued to read and learn I was surprised by how much was altered or omitted in my education about the nation. Probably started by my father's affinity for news commentaries, I became a student of United States history, especially the cold war period. In tenth-grade world history class Ms. Butler explained "manifest destiny" to us. There was no counter point to the application of the concept upon the North American continent. The 1962 film "How the West Was Won" neatly packaged Hollywood's version,

Chapter 10 - In Retrospect

entertaining though it was. I remember well Ms. Buttler explaining "caveat emptor". I thought at the time that concept seemed wrong, but I did not challenge it. We never heard about the July 1, 1917, attack on the Black neighborhood of East St. Louis Missouri, the Tulsa massacre of June 1, 1921, or of Rock Springs, Wyoming attack on immigrants of September 1885. Such incidents of racial violence were not part of our educational syllabus. It was purposefully omitted and beyond our teachers' capacity to change the culture that forced it. In effect, we had a prohibition of critical race theory sixty years before the term was created. Nevertheless, my teachers directed their efforts toward making my classmates and me informed citizens and equipping us to take advantage of our opportunities. I think they did their best within the parameters of their professional working environment.

Because we had a segregated school system there was no busing other than the city buses that carried us to our local or assigned schools. I attended Wilmore in first grade. Barringer then opened and because we lived west of Irwin Creek, I attended Barringer through third grade. We moved into the adjacent Ashley Park district, so it was Ashley Park, Spaugh and Harding. From then until graduation, we were a student family and reunited with both the Wilmore and Barringer kids who were ultimately assigned to Spaugh. Our school family seldom changed except for an occasional family that moved from or into our school district. It put a secure floor under me and my friends. It was comforting and provided stability during a time of rapid changes in our lives.

When we held our sixtieth high school class reunion a server at our venue noted his surprise that our group was so friendly and close to one another. He was almost incredulous when I explained just how long many of us have been together. My classmates were a surrogate family to me, and I remember them fondly. Very few of us were "well resourced" and those resources our families possessed were expended judiciously. It took decades for some of us to learn the difficulties other classmates experienced growing up. The lives of some were impacted by parental experiences from the Great Depression and WWII – challenges not illustrated in the scripts of *Leave It to Beaver, Ozzie and Harriet, Father Knows Best*, or *Happy Days*. Some of my classmates had to carry a lot of baggage growing up. In hindsight, I was quite fortunate.

I am proud to have been so close to my group of school pals both then and still today. We go back to 1954, a few to 1951. We tried to follow the example established for us by our parents and teachers. For my immediate pals, no one was charged with a crime and each of us has been married for decades. None of us were candidates to become sixties radicals, and we were not, although we asked a lot of questions that made adults uncomfortable – thank you Mr. Todd. We were not always satisfied accepting all we were told as truth but wanted to investigate, analyze and decide for ourselves. Our careers just might have paralleled paths our teachers would have predicted decades ago. Doing a Zoom conference with friends from seventy years ago causes me to feel I just saw them the previous day. I am indeed fortunate and blessed to have my good friends.

We were a transitional generation. We bridged between eras. One began in the late 1800s and ended in the 1960s. The other is the digital/AI era of the twentieth-first century. We had no need to process alternate realities or defend against alternate facts. We lived in a culture where political leaders and citizens alike understood there was a point at which, political differences aside, the good of the nation took precedence. We had faith in our government and nation because we were not told each day to believe otherwise. No one was afraid of being swept off a public street by masked, hooded, unidentified federal agents. We trusted our police. Our obligation was to follow what we had been taught and carry onward to preserve, protect, and enhance the nation by being loyal to its precepts and working for its future.

My friends who moved elsewhere and return to class events repeatedly tell me they do not recognize much of what they see. Those of us who remain here have difficulty comprehending Charlotte's unstoppable growth. What was once a polite, not-so-well-known city of 134,000 is now a sophisticated, upscale, and globally known new south city. In 2025 so much is happening so rapidly in so many locations. How we live drives what we build, and our urban density was unimaginable in the fifties/sixties.

An area of trees in west Charlotte that paralleled Weyland Avenue had been woods since the days of Camp Greene. The trees are gone now and replaced by multiple story apartments, shoehorned between post WWII apartments and residences. How gratifying it would be for our city to find a way to save a patch of woods here and there. Is anyone listening??

Chapter 10 - In Retrospect

Seven decades is sufficient time to replace or recycle much of Charlotte. A drive on South Tryon from Woodlawn to West Boulevard typifies many of the city's major streetscapes. Little is the same and views encapsulated in my mind do not match the views I see, even more reason to document places and adventures of what was before it is lost. The period 1950 through 1963 was a memorable time to grow up. Our many fears and uncertainties were balanced by reliable parents, friends, teachers, a stable society, and faith in the nation. There were issues that needed attention but they did not prevent Charlotte from being a comfortable refuge for young people in a much larger world of that time. The greatest threats were existential. We were living in the legacy secured by our parents' generation and its sacrifices. In an age when things were always newer, we knew things were also going to be better, and my classmates and I were told that soon we should be prepared to lead forward. The "soon" came and went. It was indeed good fortune during my professional career I had a small part in rebuilding some of the streetscapes I once walked. May God bless all my classmates and our teachers who helped us along the way.

Thank you for *Haulin' Around Town*.

Bibliography

Air Power Magazine, May 1978, Sentry Books. Airwingmedia.com. Digitized issues.

libres@uncg.edu/ir/asu/f/Dreibelbis_Vernon; a Commemorative History of Alexander Graham Junior High School. 1960

Piedmont & Northern – The Great Electric System of the South, Thomas T. Fetters/Peter W. Swanson. Golden West Books, San Marino Ca. 1974 IBSN 0-87095-051-7.

https://www.chicagorailfan.com; 1952 Mass Transit Directory.

Charlotte Magazine, June 3, 2021. Building History, Ben Douglas, Groundbreaker by Tom Hanchett. https://www.charlottemagazine.com/building-history-ben-douglas-groundbreaker/

Mayor Ben Douglas https://www.douglashistory.co.uk/history/Ben_Elbert_Douglas.html

History of J. N. Pease. Internal document.

Seaboard Motive Power, Warren L. Calloway and Paul K. Withers, Withers Publishing, Halifax, PA   1988   ISBN 0-9618503-1-0

Norfolk Southern Color Pictorial 1950s – 1970s, Dalton P. McDonald, Published by Dalton P. McDonald, 1291 Cliffwood Place, Asheboro NC 27205   2015 ISBN 978-0-692-40785-1

https://www.charlottenc.gov/files/sharedassets/city/v/1/city-government/departments/documents/clerks-office/minutes/1948-1951/minutes-1951/may-29-1951.pdf

https://www.charlottenc.gov/files/sharedassets/city/v/1/city-government/departments/documents/clerks-office/minutes/1948-1951/minutes-1950/october-4-1950.pdf

About the Author

Earl Gulledge is a war baby and was born in 1945 in Charlotte, NC. He grew up on the west side and moved to the east side of the city after marrying his wife, Emily, a former CMS teacher of 31 years, in 1970.

He attended Charlotte-Mecklenburg public schools and graduated from Harry P. Harding High School.

He holds a North Carolina architectural license and began his professional career with Charlotte's premier architecture-engineering firm, J.N. Pease Associates. In 1980, he moved to a project management role with BarclaysAmerican and later Duke Power for new/renovated administrative facilities.

Earl retired from CB Richard Ellis as a regional project manager, having spent 13 years executing work in the uptown towers along the same sidewalks he passed along as a youth. He began a parallel career as an adjunct instructor at CPCC Central Campus in 1994, a role he continues to pursue.

His interests are twentieth-century history, aviation, railroads, and US automotive history. His hobbies are model railroading and building historically accurate plastic model aircraft.

www.ingramcontent.com/pod-product-compliance
Lightning Source LLC
Chambersburg PA
CBHW071115160426
43196CB00013B/2577